Childhood Interrupted

Kathleen O'Malley

Virago

VIRAGO

First published in Great Britain in 2005 by Virago Press
Reprinted 2005 (four times), 2006 (six times)
This paperback edition published in 2006 by Virago Press
Reprinted 2006 (three times), 2007 (twice), 2008

A CIP catalogue record for this book
is available from the British Library.

ISBN 978-1-84408-118-9

Typeset in Sabon by Palimpsest Book Production Limited,
Polmont, Stirlingshire
Printed and bound in Great Britain by
Clays Ltd, St Ives plc

Virago
An imprint of
Little, Brown Book Group
100 Victoria Embankment
London EC4Y 0DY

An Hachette Livre UK Company
www.hachettelivre.co.uk

www.virago.co.uk

Kathleen O'Malley is a magistrate in Middlesex and lives in Hertfordshire. In 2005 she was voted one of Britain's bravest women by *Best* magazine.

For Mammy,
in loving memory of
the greatest mother and most courageous woman

Acknowledgements

In August 2001 I had the good fortune to meet Vincent Brown, an investigative journalist and barrister in Dublin, who highlighted my case among others and publicly vindicated my mother. I would not have been able to come on this journey without his vigorous and deeply felt support.

Thanks to Elise Dillsworth, my dear editor at Virago, who picked up on my story. Her complete belief, care, skill and dedication enabled me to fulfil my dream of publishing it.

Thanks to Maureen Paton, a wonderful journalist, who gave me my first print interview, and to Simon Mayo and Antonia Turnbull for generous time on air.

A warm thank you to all my very special friends who have given me support and encouragement: Lyn and Kenneth, Monika and Carl, Chris B., Linda, Sally and Peter, Mag and John, Christine, Shona and Mike, Shirley and Mike, Rita, Clive, Trudy, Kathy and Tom, Mike G., Bobby, Nancy, Tynna, Yvonne, Ruth, Cheryl, Michelle and Ray, Jenny and Dave, Jeremy and Denise, Edna and Don, Meir, Mary D., Jean and Eric, Laura, Ingrid and Klaus, Delia, Tony, Essie, Bridie, Brian, Paulette and

Jay, Chrissie, Chris and Michelle, Marion, Richard, Brenda, Nadia, May, Laura and Pat.

Bless you all for being there for me.

Thanks to my long-standing friends who worked with me at the Playboy Club, my new friends at line dancing classes, especially George and Barbara, 'Ginger Rogers', 'Cyd Charisse' and Helen, and my friends and colleagues on the bench.

Thanks to Jonathan and the staff at Rickmansworth Library for their assistance and willingness to help me over the past two years, and to my new friends at West Hertfordshire Golf Club.

A loving and special thank you to Steve, my husband, and our darling son Richard, for their support and encouragement when writing this book, and to my sisters and brothers and their families.

Childhood Interrupted

Prologue

I used to wonder about magistrates – what they did and how they did it, but more importantly I used to wonder *who* they were. It had always sounded such an important and highly responsible job – but it never occurred to me that I could apply to be one. As with most things in my life I took on board the details then just stored them away. I probably told myself at the time that it wasn't even worth dreaming about; becoming a Justice of the Peace just didn't happen to people like me.

In the early nineties I began to think more about it, especially when my son was about to go off to university, our dog, Tosca, was getting old, and I was starting to wonder what I was going to do with the rest of my life. I happened to meet a real magistrate and we got talking. I didn't know her well, but I was curious enough to ask her about the work she did and what the position actually entailed. Amongst other things, she said, 'You must be a pillar of society!' I thought to myself: I'm as good as anyone else. This woman was no different to me. If she could do the job so could I. I applied and in time I received an information pack, which advised reading up as much as I could about the role and also visiting my local court to sit in the gallery and see what went on. In due course this became mandatory and after a while I was asked to attend an interview. I felt totally elated. I couldn't believe this was happening to me. I talked to my husband and son and was bubbling over with excitement, but I was hiding an underlying fear that my past might rear its ugly head. This fear grew and grew, and I began to wonder if I could just say I had changed my mind rather than be turned down. So it was with very mixed feelings that I prepared for the most important interview of my life, not knowing really what was in store for me.

On the day I waited with another lady who said she came from Ealing. We talked. She was clearly middle class. I felt that the only thing we had in common was that our sons had both gone to public school. I decided within twenty seconds that she was the sort of person they were looking for; they would undoubtedly prefer her to me. In my mind she was so clearly a better candidate, I wondered what I was doing even sitting there waiting.

She was called for her interview first. I nervously sat reading the case history they had asked me to look at. After what seemed like an age it was my turn. I was called in and introduced to the three members of the committee who would be interviewing me. The letter I had received had said that I would not be expected to have any knowledge of the law or sentencing so we discussed the case history I had been given in very general terms. Then they changed tack and asked me what I would do if my son brought drugs home. I went with my instincts and just said what I'd always said – I would notify the police and with any luck a short sharp shock would stop him in his tracks. Then they asked me what I would do if I found a burglar had entered our home and injured our dog. Again not knowing if it was the right thing or not I just said if the dog was injured, I would tend to him. 'You mean you wouldn't chase after the thief?' the interviewer came back. He seemed quite surprised at this. They asked me if I did any charity work and I answered honestly that no I didn't at the present time. My son was my priority and when he left home I would engage in some kind of voluntary work. 'So you have a comfortable existence,' one of them said. I felt the interview was going rapidly downhill. But then he continued, 'But it hasn't always been like that, has it?' Immediately I started to panic. I took a deep breath to try to calm myself down. I thought to myself, Oh God! Do I have to tell them everything now? But the chairman had a kindly face and I decided to tell them the truth about things I had kept secret for the past forty-seven years.

No, it hadn't always been so comfortable, I began. I'd been raped at the age of eight and despite the fact that my mother had successfully prosecuted my attacker, I and my sisters had been taken from her and locked up for the rest of our child-hoods in an Industrial School in County Westmeath in Ireland where we were beaten and dressed in rags and worked to the bone, whilst receiving almost no education. Once I started I just couldn't stop. I told the panel that my mother had done the best she could, but she hadn't been able to prevent it. What had happened to us was typical of the so-called care system in Ireland in the 1950s and I was unutterably angry with the Irish Government, the NSPCC and Roman Catholic Church. At the end of it all, one of the interviewers, clearly surprised by the level of my outburst, asked if I had any other skeletons in my closet? Was there anything else that I wanted to talk about that could be an embarrassment to me at a later date? I replied that they knew more about me than almost anyone. I had totally exposed myself to them. I had nothing else to hide.

As the interview came to a close, I had terribly mixed feel-ings. On one hand I thought it had been intrusively intimate and on the other I thought, Gosh! I can't believe it. I've told them everything and that wasn't really so difficult. But when

I talked to my husband Steve and my son Richard about it over dinner the elation ebbed away. I remember saying there was no way I would be appointed having discussed my past in such detail. I phoned the other woman I had met there to see how she had got on. When I put the phone down it was quite clear that she had got the job and not me.

So I was stunned to receive a letter from the Lord Chancellor's office notifying me that I had been appointed a magistrate. It was April 1997, almost eighteen months after I had first applied and I had been accepted by the highest office in the land. I was over the moon.

I've been sitting on the Bench for eight years now – the age when my life changed for ever – and when I look at the people who come in front of me, I think, There go I but for the grace of God, had not opportunities presented themselves to give me a better life. And I think back to my childhood, what it was like before and after it was so brutally interrupted.

Chapter 1

They called her the Duchess. She was better dressed than most people in our area, carried herself well and spoke nicely, with a soft lilting accent. She stood out in the heart of Dublin where we lived. I can see her now in her favourite grey tweed suit, which gave her a lovely nipped-in waist, going about her business briskly and confidently, always with a nice word for anyone we passed. You could tell at a glance she hadn't been born there; there was something in the way she conducted herself that set her apart. 'There goes the Duchess': for most people it was a term of affection, but to others, those who didn't know her at all, it was tinged with a bit of envy. Sometimes it was said with sarcasm: 'Will ya look at Miss High and Mighty now! Who does she think she is with her airs and graces?

I'm only three years old when this story starts; that's as far back as I can remember. My big sister and I didn't know then how different she was because to us she was just Mammy. And she didn't think she was better than anyone, she just knew you had to keep your wits about you to survive with two kids and no Daddy around to support them. Life had never been easy for her, but she carried on regardless. 'You can't let it get to you,' she used to say to us when things weren't going our way.

She had no family of her own, no parents, no brothers or sisters – no blood relations at all – so Sarah Louise and I meant everything to her and she made sure we knew it. Every day she told us that she loved us, that we were her bonny lasses and that she'd give us the shirt off her back if we wanted it. She made up songs about us; sometimes she sang popular songs but put our names in them, which never failed to make us feel special. We walked miles across Dublin with her like this, singing songs and making up nonsense rhymes, but best of all I liked it when we got back to our street. I always felt a warm feeling inside when we got to Whitworth Bridge over the Liffey and knew that we were a few minutes off being nice and snug at home with our shoes off and the kettle on the fire. Soon enough we were back on our street and one of the neighbours would say, 'Aren't the girls looking gorgeous now! Look at little Kathleen with her ribbons there!' And Mammy would look pleased at the compliment and say something friendly back.

Twenty-nine Lower Bridge Street, my home for the first few years of my life, wasn't really on Lower Bridge Street at all: it was on a little lane which turned off that street and it didn't have a name of its own. We lived in a tenement house just as you turned into the lane and we shared it with six other families. Though Mammy always said she'd prefer to be in one of the little white corporation cottages down the lane, but to me our building seemed much better with its grand, dark front and numerous windows. When you went in through the worn and chipped dark red front door, which no one ever locked, there was a wide central communal staircase. It was always very dark in the stairway, so my sister and I used to rush up the steps, two at a time, before the bogey man could get us.

When you got to the second floor, we were on the left of

the landing and our neighbour Mrs Harris and her family were on the right. We had two rooms: the front room had the coal fire, the stove for cooking and Mammy's bed tucked over in one corner; the back room had the big iron bed that my sister and I slept in. We liked Mammy's room the most because it was the cosiest. When we came home from our errands, we used to light the fire and sit in front of it warming ourselves, while Mammy got our dinner on the stove.

Once a week we would get the tin bath out from under her bed, Mammy would heat up lots of kettles of water and we would all have a lovely, warm, soapy bath. When we came out we'd be wrapped in towels and Mammy would cuddle us in front of the fire whilst she told us stories about olden times, leprechauns, fairies, banshees and Grania O'Malley, who was a famous Irish warrior. The best bit was when she used to twirl her fingers in my blond hair and tell me I was like one of the princesses and I would want that bit to go on for ever. Sometimes after the bath we sat at our little wooden table where we had our meals and did drawing and looked at picture books till sleep time. But Mammy would also take us to the public baths once a month. She had to pay for these baths but it was great fun to have running hot water, to splash around and make noise.

Our bed had the Sacred Heart at one end and the Virgin Mary opposite. We slept top-to-toe in there and took it in turns which way we were facing. There was no heating at all in our room and if it was a particularly cold night, Mammy would put our coats on top of the blankets to give us some extra warmth. Most days though, I did my best to go to sleep in Mammy's bed. I liked to doze off watching the dying glow of the fire and Mammy knitting or quietly getting on with her chores. In that room I would drift off into the loveliest sleep but could never work out how I managed to wake up in my own bed in the morning.

We had a gas meter and there was a little pile of coins on

the mantelpiece to feed it. You could tell when it was going to run out because the lights started to flicker and then one or other of us would rush over, stand on the kitchen chair and put the change in. Like the rest of the families in Lower Bridge Street, we got our water from the standpipe outside in the lane; no one had anything as grand as a tap or running water inside their houses. Although there was sometimes a queue with twenty or so families sharing the same supply, we were entirely used to it, it was part of our life. And, similarly, we all shared a toilet which was also outside down the lane. At night we made our own arrangements. There was no way any of us were getting out of our warm beds, putting our coats on and going down to the privy when it was blackness outside, so we put up with having a wee in the bucket and emptying it out in the morning.

Once the fire was lit, the first chore of the morning was emptying out the night bucket and filling up the kettle from the tap. Often when we were little Mammy had to make a couple of journeys to get the water for all our needs – washing, drinking and cooking. Once we were old enough to go to the standpipe for ourselves we seemed to spend a lot of time lugging water around either for Mammy or for one of the other families in the lane. We all helped each other out.

You could tell she hadn't been born and bred in Dublin like the vast majority of our neighbours because she didn't wear the grey shawl round her shoulders like they did. If you walked down our lane, or any of the roads around us, you'd see the doorways were full of women talking, gossiping, sharing a bit of a scandal, cradling their babies in that unmistakable grey rug. Mammy looked totally different to them. Where she came from, the women didn't drape bits of wool round themselves; blankets were for the bedroom and that was where they stayed. She was looked upon as a country woman – a culchie – as different from the Dubliners as it was possible to be. She didn't sound like them either – she had been brought up on a farm and had a refined, gentle voice, without a trace of the harsh vowels of the women she chatted to. But those years in the country had done more than just shape how she sounded; they had moulded her personality as well. She had an extremely sunny disposition; she was outgoing and sociable and talked to everyone, young and old. And although she was an outsider, there is no doubt she was well liked. People called out to her all the time when we walked down the lane and her face always lit up when she greeted them. She wasn't one of them, but she was in no way a country bumpkin either; she was quite a mystery, the Duchess. Occasionally she would get drawn into a dispute, and someone would try to claim her for their side and she would just say lightly, with a smile on her face, 'I'm half culchie and half Dublin now: I'm both of you!'

In the winter our lane became a muddy skating rink, its potholes filled with puddles. Every day the mud from Lower Bridge Street was trampled up our stairs and into our two rooms despite Mammy's best efforts. We tried to wipe our shoes at the door as we had been told but it seemed to come in anyway. Every day Mammy got down on her hands and knees and scrubbed the floors in our two rooms in a desperate attempt to keep them clean. She put newspaper over the wet bits so that we had somewhere to walk whilst it dried. Sometimes she tackled the main stairwell as well with her bucket and scrubbing brush and sheets of old newspaper placed like stepping stones. Tramps who had nowhere else to go used to come in at night and sleep in our hallway because our front door was never locked. Mammy was always very sympathetic towards these people and used to say that being inside, even in an unheated entrance hall, was better than being out there under the stars. Sometimes they were still there in the morning and Mammy would just wash around them, careful not to disturb their rest. If either of us so much as sniggered under our breath about those piles of rags kipping in our hallway, Mammy would silence us with a look that threatened the wrath of God and all else besides.

Mammy always worked. She cleaned at home and she cleaned for other people. She cleaned hotels and hospitals and private houses, but she only took jobs where we could go along with her. We had to sit quiet as mice and not be any trouble whilst she did her work. She was paid in cash, a few shillings here and there, and it lived in a pot on the mantelpiece. If there was a bit of money left over once she'd paid the rent, fed the meter and bought the food, she would buy me and my sister ribbons for our hair. Sarah Louise had long straight dark hair, and I had thick, unruly blond hair with a mind of its own. I hated having my hair combed. I would run around the table with Mammy trying to catch me. But every day she brushed and plaited or turned it into ringlets with ribbons on and sent us off into the world looking and feeling like the princesses we read about in books. That feeling didn't last long though. We didn't realise it then but we lived in the poorest, most deprived part of Dublin and those ribbons were lucky if they made it to the end of our street, let alone the end of the day without someone robbing them off our heads and then running off. But Mammy never gave up. When she got a bit more money she went back to the market and got us some more. She felt that these little details were very important to how you felt about yourself. She thought that looking smart mattered and if she expected us to look smart, then she must too. In our two little rooms with the outside tap, she kept us all well groomed and respectably turned out.

She went to the hairdresser from time to time to get her fine hair cut and styled. One time she came back very upset: she'd had a wave put in and it hadn't worked. Her usually soft, pretty hair was now all frizzy and fried-looking and she was inconsolable. I was very young but deeply conscious of the fact that our strong, capable mammy had been reduced to tears by this horrible treatment called a permanent wave. Sarah Louise and I were torn between wanting to comfort her and wanting to touch this thing on her head, where her hair used to be, which felt like a nest of coarse, crisp straw.

When life did threaten really to get on top of her, or the distillery next door was belching out particularly horrible smells, she would close the windows and we would all go out for a 'constitutional'. The distillery was behind us, but it towered over our home like a giant belching out its stinky breath. It really bothered Mammy, who said that the air in Dublin was dirty and smoky enough anyway without having 'that pollution' added to it. We'd never known anything different, but she had grown up in the Dublin Mountains, breathing the fresh country air, and was horrified by the thought of what she was subjecting her children to: she was very concerned about our health living in the city.

Every morning after breakfast we were given a big spoonful of malt and cod liver oil combined. It was for our well-being, she said, to make our skin clear and our bones strong. Mammy had been raised on it and she'd scarcely had a day's sickness in her life. I didn't mind what it did, it tasted lovely: sweet, black and treacly. With that in our tummies, Mammy would button us into our coats and take us out into the fresh air. She was a great believer in the healing power of a good walk.

We lived in the middle of the city right next to the Brazen Head, the oldest pub in all of Dublin. We were surrounded by churches and pubs. 'God and the Devil!' she used to say with a laugh – you couldn't go a hundred yards without tripping over one or the other. Mammy loved the churches, the sound of the bells when they all pealed at once, and we went to Mass every Sunday. But the pubs she would have nothing to do with. She swept us past their doorways and told us not to look inside. Yet she liked the vibrancy and colour of the city. We always joined in after Mass on St Patrick's Day when there was a huge procession through the streets of Dublin and the bagpipes would play and everyone would be dressed up in their Sunday best. Sarah Louise and I decided we loved St Patrick, whoever he was, he must have been a nice man, because suddenly everyone was in a good mood, patting us on the head and giving us sweets.

We regularly walked over to St Stephen's Green, near the Shelbourne Hotel which Mammy used to clean. It was quite a way there from our house and since Mammy was very friendly and stopped to talk to everyone it took us quite a while just to get away from Lower Bridge Street what with babies to coo at and neighbours to catch up with. I loved these trips out in my smartly pressed clothes, with ribbons in my hair and Mammy saying hello to everyone. But it was particularly good when we finally got to the Green because there was a pond and we would throw bread to the ducks and afterwards we would run around on the grass. One time I was so fascinated by the ducks and their antics I slipped down the steep mossy side and fell in. Mammy had to come and rescue me, which wasn't difficult because it was quite shallow, but the walk back home again wasn't very comfortable, me dripping with water and smelling of pond weed. By the end of the week people down the lane were saying that the little blonde one had nearly drowned. Gossip travelled fast and imaginatively!

When the weather was good we went to the seaside. Mammy loved fresh air – she had grown up with it – and whenever we could we would go to the Bull Wall at Dollymount, Port Marnock or Malahide. Dollymount was a real favourite but it was a long way out of Dublin, across the Liffey, five or six miles at least. We would pack up a picnic and take the bus excited as anything. But if the bus was late, Mammy would just announce that we would do the remaining miles on foot, hardly noticing the distance with the imminent promise of sand between our toes and a paddle in the sea. More often than not my best friend Chrissie Dumphy would come along too and Chrissie would be so happy she would shout, 'We're going on holiday, we're going on holiday,' all the way out there to anyone who cared to listen.

Dollymount was on the northern outskirts of Dublin and the nearest thing that you could call a resort near to where we lived. There was a rocky section down one end where you could lower yourself down some steep steps into the deep sea. We always stuck to the sandy bit; none of us could swim and there in the shallows, we could mess around to our heart's content. We built huge sandcastles and decorated them with shells and bits of seaweed. Mammy always let her hair down and joined in with our games, chasing us and burying us in the sand.

Mammy never liked excluding people. Pied-Piper-style she would gather up whoever was available whenever we were having a day out. There was a local boy called Paddy May and his cousin Kathleen who regularly used to come with us; she had always liked Paddy despite the fact that he was a bit older than us and had a reputation for being the local scallywag. He and his cousin lived in St Audoens, the block of corporation flats across the road. Everyone aspired to these; they were owned by the council and the Mays were considered very fortunate to have one. Paddy spent very little time actually in his house though; he was always out in the lane running around, playing practical jokes on people and trying to peep up our skirts. Mammy always said he was a good boy really and had a kind heart underneath it all.

Mammy loved kids. She loved making things special for them. Birthdays were a big thing for her and she saved up money in the jar when one of ours was coming up. When it was your birthday you were allowed to choose the colour of icing for your cake. There were only a few colours, but the main thing was we were given a choice and mine was always pink. In the morning she made jellies as well and these were put out on to the small window sill in our bedroom to set. Sometimes we would have an impromptu birthday party and she would take the His Master's Voice gramophone – her pride and joy – down to the lane where we'd listen to a few records, have a hooley and everyone would join in. Mammy would encourage us to sing and dance and if we were very lucky she would start to yodel. She was a great entertainer and no one could resist her when she started up. Afterwards we went back up to our house for birthday cake and coconut sandwich biscuits and three-quarters-set jelly.

Chapter 2

Mammy's own childhood had been disrupted by war and her family had been driven apart. As a result her memories were fractured and hazy. She was born Mary O'Malley, later known as May, in Dublin in 1919. She had an older brother but she could remember little about him. As a very young girl she had been separated from her family because of the Civil War. Her earliest memory was that 'some sort of fighting had broken out' and she was 'lost' by her mother and father and brother. Those were the very words she used. She was very vague about what had caused the family to split up and I knew better than to delve too deeply. But I later read more about this period in Irish history and discovered that a lot of families were fragmented by the sectarian fighting, which went on for years after Ireland officially became a Free State in the early 1920s. People faced bitter differences even within their own community; many fled not only the area they had grown up in, they fled Ireland itself. It may have been political upheaval or it may have been personal upheaval which forced my mother's family to scatter in different directions; but the end result was that my mother was placed in St Anne's Orphanage in Dublin.

She never managed to piece together those first years of her life, in fact she never really tried. She did not talk much about this early part of her life: the past was the past and probably best left like that. One of the only things she did recall from that time at the orphanage was a lady in black, always very elegantly dressed, who used to visit her but then suddenly stopped doing so. Mammy did not know who this visitor in mourning was. All she could remember were the beautiful clothes worn by this lady, who may or may not have been her mother, and her loneliness when she stopped coming to see her. We always looked sad when she got to the bit about being all on her own in the orphanage but she said it was quite a nice place and not so horrible really. I later found out that in those days orphanages were fee-paying, private institutions, which offered an alternative to families who had suffered a change of circumstances. The fact that she was cared for in such a place might indicate that her parents were middle class, which would explain her accent and rather refined way of doing things. But at the age of six, her life changed again. Perhaps the smartly dressed lady also died, and with the money no longer coming in, the orphanage did what they did with any child who no longer had a family: they fostered her out – to Mr and Mrs Murphy, who had a large family. They were comfortably off, had a nice home and, as good Catholics, wanted to share that with someone less fortunate than themselves. They lived in the mountains in a place called Bohernabreena, about fourteen miles south-west of Dublin. The first few years of Mammy's life there were relatively carefree; she attended the local school along with the Murphy girls and when she came home, joined in with life as a farm girl, caring for the hens and chickens, gradually learning to be at ease with the animals and in the end to ride the horses bareback as well as the best of them. But all that changed when Mrs Murphy died unexpectedly when my mother was ten years old. Overnight, she was expected to take over the female role around the house, to run the place and keep it clean and tidy. They had no other domestic help and someone had to step into Mrs Murphy's shoes. The boys were out milking the cows, looking after the land, dealing with the farm work and she was left to carry out the housework.

She continued to go to school and when she came home, cleaned, tidied and made the tea for the men, when they came in from the milking. For a few more months, she attended the local school with the brother, a boy called Terry, who had become her best friend in the family, but at the age of eleven, her domestic role took over.

Mrs Murphy's death brought my mother's childhood to an abrupt end. For the next ten years she worked hard to look after the family – and then disaster struck. This young girl whom they had 'rescued' from the orphanage, brought into the bosom of the family and treated as if she were their own, repaid them by becoming pregnant! Ten years was as nothing: she had brought shame and disgrace on the family and she was told to leave the farm and never to come back again. Nobody bothered to ask her who the father was and what he had to say for himself.

My mother was sent away to have her baby on her own and finally gave birth to my older sister, Sarah Louise, at a hospital in Dublin before going to live in a place called the Regina Coeli which was a well-known home for unmarried mothers. She was twenty years old.

In those days there were few greater crimes a woman could commit than to have a child outside of holy wedlock. Mammy must have been a determined character because she managed to keep Sarah Louise when most illegitimate children born in Ireland in the forties and fifties were taken straight from their mother at birth. She had hardly any money and earned what little she could by helping the nuns look after the babies in the nursery; for a few months that was how she got by. But she knew she couldn't stay there for ever. If she wanted to keep the child, she had to get out and that is how she came to live in the slums of Dublin, along with the poorest of the poor.

She rented a room in Dublin and when she went out to work she took Sarah Louise along in her pram. At times, though, she couldn't make enough to pay for her lodging so she would move back into the Regina Coeli and help out in the nursery until she was on her feet again.

Eighteen months after Sarah Louise's birth, Mammy discovered she was pregnant again, with me. My father – whoever he was – was nowhere to be seen. To have another mouth to feed would not be easy. She could have chosen to have a back-street abortion as others did; such things were possible even at that time if she could have scraped together enough money. She could have given me up for adoption. Instead she chose neither of these options, she chose the hardest of all: to hang on to her baby. But by choosing to keep me, she chose a life of even greater hardship and public shame than the one she already had.

I was born on 26 March 1942 in the Rotunda Hospital in Dublin and she called me Kathleen. On my birth certificate, the box where my father's name should be was left blank, just as it was on my sister's.

I have often wondered who my father was. I was given no clues. Perhaps it was someone at one of her places of employment – the head of the household or one of the sons? Perhaps it was someone she fell head over heels in love with? To this day I do not know; Mammy never would tell, except to say, 'He was a nice kind man.' Even when we were all much older, the right moment to ask never seemed to arrive. Perhaps I had the same father as Sarah Louise, though there are few physical similarities between us. My father remained an absence, a white space on a form, never spoken of.

Within days my mother was taken in again by the Regina Coeli home, along with her two little girls. She was allowed to recuperate for a short time but that was all. Nothing was free and after a week or so under their roof, she was told she had to work if she wanted to stay. What else could she do? She had to stay. It was impossible for a woman nursing a tiny baby with a two-year-old child in tow as well to gain employment in the outside word so Mammy went back to work in the nursery. She loved looking after other people's babies but it must have been very hard for her emotionally. Most of the babies in the nursery would not be staying with their birth mothers. The poor women gave birth, the babies stayed in the nursery for a while, before being whisked away and adopted by a couple who would hopefully be able to give them a good and loving home. There is no doubt she must have witnessed some harrowing scenes when the mothers realised their babies had gone for good. For somebody in my mother's position, fighting to hold on to her own babies, it must have been a very traumatic place to work, but perhaps it is what gave her the stamina and tenacity for the battles which lay ahead.

She worked hard at the home and in time she managed to put enough by to get a place of her own. It was nothing grand but at least it was somewhere she could call home. She managed to scratch together enough furniture to make it comfortable. It was increasingly hard to find jobs which would let her bring two little girls along and there were times when she was forced to go back and spend periods of time at the home for unmarried mothers. When she was four years old Sarah Louise contracted tuberculosis and had to be cared for in hospital for six months as she convalesced. We were in and out and in and out of hospital each day for her treatment. It was impossible for Mammy to work with my big sister so ill, so we left our rooms in the tenements and went back to stay in the Regina Coeli.

It was not a comfortable place. We all slept in one long room, like an old-fashioned hospital ward. There was no privacy. The nuns had their cells, but it was out of the question for the likes of us to be given a room. Mammy and I would sleep top-to-tail in one bed, surrounded by similar little huddles. One of my earliest memories comes from that stay in the home. I was sitting in the bath and a nun was washing me and she said, 'Oh, what beautiful skin you have.' I was about two years old and she made a big impression on me with her starched habit and sweet face. It was not an unhappy time; we had a roof over our head, shelter and warmth and the kindly nuns took care of us. Best of all I had Mammy to myself.

We weren't in there very long. As soon as my sister's health was restored we had to fall back on our own resources, this time in two rooms which were to become our home for the next few years: 29 Lower Bridge Street. And once we were on our feet again we made one of many trips to visit the Murphys. Even though they had scorned her Mammy still returned in the hope of being accepted back. We used to go out to the farm whenever we could, usually by long and complicated pre-arrangement, letters going back and forth about what time we were arriving. It was thirteen miles from where we lived to Bohernabreena, a long way to travel in those days. We went out by bus to Aylesbury in Tallaght or the Dublin Mountains, then we would walk for miles and miles until we got to a special meeting place where we would sit and wait for Uncle Terry and his pony and trap to take us up to the farm. I always remember the weather being nice, warm and sunny, and we loved being in the open air listening for Uncle Terry whose arrival was announced by the clip-clopping sound of the pony's hooves.

It always seemed like a wonderful adventure was about to

start when our uncle appeared on the horizon. He had a lovely, smiling face and he always looked so pleased to see us. He would jump down off the pony and, holding its reins, help us on to the trap. We climbed up the steps at the back and sat on two little benches facing each other. The steps folded up under themselves and then we were off, bumping gently along the country roads.

Mammy always made a very special effort for these visits to Bohernabreena. She spent ages getting us ready and we always had to look the same. One time she bought us matching Fair Isle jumpers on the weekly payment, another time there were red dresses she had knitted specially, with red ribbons threaded through the waist. She would put on her smart grey suit and tie her hair back with a bow or a clasp. She wanted her adopted family to see how well she was doing raising her girls; she always set out with very high hopes.

On the way there she talked to us about her life growing up in the country. It seemed to hold many treasured memories for her. There had been lots of horses on the farm and she had learnt to ride without a saddle from an early age. She could get on a horse – any horse – and ride it with total confidence. The children were nice to her but Uncle Terry she was particularly close to. She had been responsible for taking him to school and there was a strong bond between them. Mammy always looked so happy when she talked about those times, and we could never hear enough of it.

Sometimes – for no reason at all – we just waited and waited in vain by the roadside for the familiar sound of Uncle Terry's arrival. Hours later, with a look of defeat that she would do her best to hide, Mammy would just say, 'Let's go home now, darlings.'

Other times when Uncle Terry didn't show up we would walk the long distance to the homestead by ourselves and it would take us over an hour. Sometimes we weren't even asked into the farm itself.

But to my mother those visits out to the farm were worth it because the Murphys were like family to her; the only family she could really remember. And she loved just being back in the countryside again, the outdoors, the wind in her hair. She spent most of her life cooped up in two rooms in the inner city, surrounded by drunkards and pubs and fumes from the distillery. No wonder that farm meant so much to her, it was everything our life in the tenement wasn't, and we kept on going back.

Chapter 3

Mammy made the best of it but there is no doubt life was hard for her, working every hour she could, struggling to find enough money to get by. But when I was two years old all that changed: she met the man she would later marry. His name was Thomas Byrne and Tommy, as we were asked to call him, was different. He told her stories about his job for the Postal Service, working on the mailboats that frequently took him overseas to England carrying letters back and forth, and she told him about us, our games together, our life in Lower Bridge Street. Amazingly enough he was not put off by this woman with two fatherless children, who scratched a living from cleaning jobs. In fact her stories had quite the opposite effect: he admired her spirit and liked her sense of liveliness.

I was three years old when Mammy married Tommy Byrne and suddenly there was light at the end of the tunnel. He came from a family of civil servants and they were very well respected. He was away a lot, but he always sent a postal order back to us and suddenly Mammy had a regular income, which meant we would never have to seek temporary refuge in the Regina

Coeli again. Mammy was happy, so we were happy, but I do remember the slightest niggling worry that he might take her away from us. Sarah Louise and I had taken it in turns to share her bed and suddenly there was a man around with a better claim on it than we had. I had never known a 'daddy', had never known to miss one, and suddenly my little universe of girls' things and dollies felt rather threatened. But I needn't have worried. Tommy's work kept him away for long periods of time and when he came back he was very nice, so gentle with us that it was worth giving up Mammy for a few days. After a while we started to count off the days till he came back but he worked hard, long hours and numerous shifts on the boats, and, though he supported us, we saw very little of him at Lower Bridge Street.

In July 1945, Lydia, my little sister, was born. She was a lovely baby: she had a mass of natural tight curls like Shirley Temple and a sweet and easy temperament. Sarah Louise and I took it in turns playing with her and singing and, as she grew older, wrapping her up in a blanket and taking her down to the lane to show her off to the other children. When Tommy was home we would walk down the street together with Lydia smiling out from her pram and people would say, 'Hello there, Mr and Mrs Byrne.' I remember feeling that we were a proper family at last and that nothing could touch us. Even though we weren't Tommy's real children he made it clear that he made no distinction between his own daughter, Lydia, and us. He was our daddy too. He was the sort of man who liked to do things properly and he told us that it was his intention to adopt my sister and me legally. He was making a start on the necessary paperwork.

It was a happy time. I remember one particular day vividly. We were on O'Connell Bridge, my mother, smartly dressed as always, was holding Lydia in her arms, I was on one side, my sister on the other, and a street photographer came up and snapped us. He said, 'Them's three gorgeous daughters you've got there, Missus,' and persuaded Mammy to buy it by flattering her and being charming. We had been taken out shopping that day for a treat and I remember saying to her, 'Mammy, why don't you buy something for yourself – you never buy anything just for you!' She just laughed and dismissed it and said she didn't need anything. She had everything she wanted and any extra money she had went on us. She had opened accounts for the three of us recently at the Post Office round the corner from where we lived and when she did have a few spare halfpennies we were allowed to go and deposit them in our accounts. Sarah Louise and I had little concept of money but we went down there so regularly, we were convinced that we were well on the way to being the richest girls in the city.

Like every good Catholic family, rich or poor, we went to Church every Sunday to hear Mass. After the service we went to St Stephen's Green for an ice cream. That was our treat and in my opinion it was the best ice cream in all Ireland! Mammy wasn't a particularly God-fearing woman, despite saying her prayers every day, but she did have a great respect for the Catholic Church and the traditions it upheld. In her eyes a religious upbringing could save you from the drunken, thieving misery we saw on a daily basis. When it came to the question of schooling there was little debate for her. Although John's Lane School was close to where we lived and where the majority of local parents sent their children, it just didn't feel right to her. It was run by the Augustine Brothers but the actual teaching was done by lay teachers rather than by the religious themselves. We walked past the school gates daily and saw the kids come flying out, boys and girls together, wild and reckless, laughing and swearing, with no regard for Mammy and the little one in the pram. She became more and more resolved that the atmosphere was too rough and tumble for her little girls; it wasn't the place for us at all.

Mammy had received very little schooling herself and she was determined that things would be different for us. She became convinced that George's Hill, which was a convent school about twenty minutes' walk away, was the right school to provide us with a good education. It was run by the nuns and therefore, as far as Mammy was concerned, was everything that John's Lane was not. It was a typical convent day school, an impressive Georgian building with large windows and wrought-iron railings outside. It had been founded by a woman who wanted to help educate the children of the poor of Dublin. There were two entrances to the school: one for the children, with a separate wing each for the boys and the girls; and another to the convent for the nuns. It was quite a deep building, a labyrinth of small rooms with a courtyard out at the back. The classes were very large though the boys and girls were taught separately.

Every day we walked the twenty minutes or so to school and every day we came home for lunch and then went back again. Now Lydia was old enough to be left with a neighbour, Mammy had resumed some of her cleaning jobs. There was always a meal waiting for us when we ran up the stairs at midday: pigs' trotters, boiled beef and cabbage, a bit of ham; sometimes a bowl of delicious nettle soup which she had learnt to make at the farm. The main course varied, but afterwards it was always the same: a bowl of creamy rice pudding. Then we went back off to George's Hill for the afternoon. At the end of the day, when we got home for tea, we had a slice of white bread with a generous sprinkling of sugar on top, which you had to eat carefully because the sugar spilled off if there was no dripping to hold it in place. All the kids in Dublin had that if they were lucky enough; the sugar was for energy and the bread was to put a bit of covering on your bones. We used to argue over who would get the ends of the bread – the heel or 'cat's skin' – as this had a different and nicer taste to the rest of the loaf.

In the evenings we would sing. Mammy would wind up the gramophone player, put on one of her 78s – country and western music or her all-time favourite, Slim Whitman – and we would sing along. We sang classical songs and pop songs; 'How Much is that Doggy' and 'Danny Boy'; we had quite a range. Mammy had such a beautiful voice and I loved it when she sang 'I'll take you home again, Kathleen' especially for me. Mammy had one particular song that she was fond of and she used to sing it to us all the time. 'There were three lovely lasses from Banyon, Banyon, Banyon, and you' – pointing at one or other of us – 'are the best of them all.' It didn't matter that she rotated whose turn it was; when *you* were selected, you felt that you were the most special little girl in the world. Mammy would hum the 'Blue Danube' to herself and her face took on a dreamy and faraway expression. When we thought she was out of earshot, Sarah Louise and I came up with our own lyrics, 'It's all on your leg, Gick, Gick, La La', and then we would fall about laughing at our own brilliance.

Having a stepdaddy, even if he was away a lot, gave us a financial security we had never had before and it also gave me and my sister a new-found confidence, but it was very short-lived. Before Tommy's wish to formally adopt us could be granted, our lives were to take a tragic downward turn.

Since their marriage the money from Tommy's pay cheque had arrived on a Monday morning as regular as clockwork. We would hear the telegraph boy shouting out in the lane, Letter for Mrs Byrne, Mrs Byrne!' And Mammy would rush down to collect it. Then suddenly the money stopped coming and Mammy couldn't understand it. At first Mammy just put it down to bad luck and we somehow managed to scratch by. Then, when a few more payments went the same way, she started to blame my stepfather. She told us one night when we were sitting by the fire that he had seemed like a man in a million to her but really he was the same as all the other

Irishmen she knew. We hadn't had any money coming in the post for weeks now and Mammy said we'd be back in the Regina Coeli at this rate.

When our stepfather made his next visit home she was very cross with him. Tommy looked totally surprised by what she was accusing him of but instead of getting angry, just said he could check at the post office to see what the problem was. When he did so he found that the money had arrived at our home but for the last few weeks it had been intercepted by our downstairs neighbour – Mr McCabe – who had said that he would pass it on, only he never did. From this point on, all I know for sure is that Tommy went to accuse our neighbour of stealing the money and he never came home again. The next time I saw him was at the mortuary. Somehow the confrontation had ended in his death.

The following days went by in a haze. My mother wept and wept, and the sight of her made Sarah Louise and me cry too. I didn't really understand what death was, that Tommy had gone for ever, but I did know that I couldn't bear to see my mother so sad.

I remember little of the funeral, apart from Mammy crying again when she saw the coffin with my stepfather's body in it being placed in the black carriage. I do recall the horses, two beautiful big black mares with their plumes of feathers and shining brasses which she had paid for to pull the hearse. We walked along behind them as they made their way from the church to the cemetery where he was to be buried. Now Mammy was keeping her emotions tightly in check, until the terrible moment when they lowered the coffin into the ground – *ashes to ashes, dust to dust* – and she started to sob again, loudly. The rest of the time we just stood there, me, Mammy, Sarah Louise and Lydia, holding hands, still as statues.

Afterwards, Mammy never seemed to stop crying. Tommy had been the only man in her life to be true to his word. He had represented everything good in her life. The love and security, the promise of a happy future for her and her children that he had provided had now been senselessly taken away. Everything that would have given her a respectable life had simply vanished into thin air. Now Mammy was on her own again, her solitude even more terrible for having known Tommy's support, and she was going to have to fight harder than ever to survive. What she didn't realise at the time was that it didn't matter what she did, it would never be enough to save us.

Chapter 4

Sarah Louise and I were as different as chalk and cheese. She was a tomboy – a rebel who preferred playing with balls to playing with dolls. She did not care what she looked like: she would scuff her shoes mucking about with her friends in the lane and they would stay scuffed until Mammy took her in hand. I, by contrast, was something of a mummy's girl – never doing anything I hadn't been given permission to do; immaculate and fussy, I liked pretty things and dollies and to Sarah Louise I probably seemed a bit like one myself. My sister had her own set of friends and to me they seemed unreachably glamorous and grown up. Although I would not have dared to do half the things they did, I longed to be asked to join in their games. But at four years old, I was far too young to be taken seriously, so was left to play my dolly games by myself.

Across the landing from us lived Mrs Harris who had only one room and six children and they all shared the same bed. As if there weren't enough people in there, Mrs Harris often had her nieces over for the day and they were the same ages as me and my sister. In time we became very good friends with those girls: Sarah Louise played with Margaret Dumphy, the eldest, and I played with Chrissie.

It was just as well I had Chrissie because I was never good enough for Sarah Louise. Although Mammy did everything she could to make sure that we played properly there was little that she or anyone could have done to bring us together. Although she insisted we had equal share of the bicycle, as soon as we were outside in the lane and Mammy wasn't looking, my sister would 'share' with her friends and I would be left out. It always caused the most tremendous arguments. It was the same when Mammy gave us some roller skates. I was so happy – they were the best ones around at the time; a metal frame which you could adjust to any shoe size. As long as you remembered to do the nuts up tightly you could just fly down the street in them. But if you didn't tighten them up they started to grow bigger as you went along and then the world became a very wobbly place until you skidded to a halt or fell flat on your face scraping your knees and hands.

The bike was really a tricycle. It had a big front wheel and two small rear ones and together with the roller skates formed a dynamic pair of conveyances to take us places we had hitherto only dreamed of. To get to the shops on Thomas Street you had to walk up a long steep hill. Coming down John's Lane on roller skates had to be one of the best feelings ever. In time we used to come down that hill in an old pram, which in Dublin were used like shopping trolleys. Such prams might have started life as a beautiful Silver Cross for a precious first baby, but because they were used over and over again, the hoods would go missing, the mattresses would fall apart, they would spend a few years carting the shopping to and fro before finding their real vocation in life: a go-kart with a small child inside to be sent scooting down a hill, in theory to be caught by the person at the bottom. Boxes on wheels were used for much the same thing. Whatever we could find we would turn into games: a bicycle wheel without a tyre could be sped along by working it with a stick; we climbed up the lamp-posts and tied ropes above the ledges, then used them as a swing; we chalked out a rough course and threw an old shoe polish tin down, filled with sand or stones to give it weight, and did hopscotch wherever and whenever.

One of our favourite games was hitching a ride on the back of the Guinness cart. It was a very familiar sight to us, laden down with Guinness barrels, doing its deliveries. It would come past the end of our road on its way to the Brazen Head and the pub across the road. The drayman sat on the front, with a long whip in one hand and the reins in the other. We would then jump on the back, holding on by our fingertips, while we tucked our legs and bodies underneath the cart. If the drayman thought he had a stowaway he would shout, 'Feck off!' in irritation and crack his whip back over the cart to try to dislodge us. The challenge was to duck the drayman's whip and get as close to home as possible before we leapt off and legged it.

I tried to think up games that Sarah Louise would like, games with balls, games involving a bit of daring, but the truth quickly dawned on me that she just preferred playing with *other* people. She was feisty, clever, streetwise and tougher than me by miles. Mammy used to get angry with her when she seemed to be running wild and much as I longed to be part of her set, I did not dare upset Mammy in any way. I was secretly in awe of my big, brave older sister but it didn't come out like that. I used to tell tales on her to Mammy. When she came back at me eyes blazing, aware that I had told on her, I used to say, 'Oh, leave me alone, I've got a headache,' and she would just give me that withering look which only an older sister can really master, a look of pure animosity. We weren't friends, we co-existed together; my dolls in one corner of the room, her balls in the other, the roller skates in the middle; the rivalry was intense. At the end of each day we would haul our toys up two flights of stairs. We had learnt never to leave anything out in the lane or in the hallway. If you did leave your things unattended for even a few minutes, someone would rob them, like as not.

Most days after school we went to the Iveagh building, in Bull Alley, which provided a cup of cocoa and a bun for all the children from the Liberties, as we were known. (The Liberties was the name given to our run-down area of the inner city.) It was an act of philanthropy that had been instituted by the Guinness brewing family, who owned one of the biggest businesses in the whole of Ireland and who felt honour bound to give back to those less fortunate in the city. For us children it was like an after-school club and we all loved it. It was known locally as the Beano – pronounced Bayno. We raced along there after school to be first in the queue. Boys and girls did not mix and queued up first on alternate days, but everybody got served, you never went without. We ate in a huge, high-ceilinged room with white tiles and green borders and after tea the lay teachers taught us drawing, sewing and other feminine activities whilst the boys did gym and exercises in the other room or in the courtyard. It was a noisy, happy place and we all thought the Guinness family was wonderful.

Mammy was very keen for us to learn traditional Irish dancing and since you could also do that at the Beano, whenever she had a bit of extra money she paid for my sister and me to learn. Once a week a short, plump lady called Miss O'Reilly would teach us the steps – 'Hands by your sides now, girls, backs straight, no giggling' – and we would stampede across the floor like a herd of wildebeest, desperately trying to remember the right moves. When Miss O'Reilly showed us herself how to do it, suddenly she wasn't a middle-aged lady any more; she was sixteen years old, light as a feather and she was flying. I loved watching her dance so upright, her feet tapping to the music. It was the one thing that Sarah

Louise and I could agree on: Irish dancing was just the best thing in the world. Privately I also came to the conclusion that it was the one thing – the only thing – that I was better at than her.

There was another place which provided for families who lived in the Liberties though it couldn't have been more different. It was a religious charity set up to help the poor and needy of Ireland. It had a soup kitchen and used to serve a hot meal in the middle of the day. In theory you could also go to them if you needed furniture or things for the house which you just could not afford; in theory they would take a note of your circumstances and provide you with what you lacked. The practice was very different. I remember Mammy going to them about some blankets since ours were nearly worn through and being humiliated, literally made to beg, before they would do anything. I saw Mammy struggle to stop the tears from coming and I hated them for it. Afterwards she said it was one of the most degrading things she had ever done and she would rather use the coats piled on top of the bed as we had been doing. But in the months after Tommy died she had to bite her tongue and went back quite a few times for items that had broken and we hadn't money to replace.

Mammy believed that you should always treat people decently irrespective of where they had come from. She was a very fair person but she could be quite strict. She did not allow any bad behaviour or fighting; there was a special no-nonsense look which she kept for such occasions. If Chrissie Dumphy and I were having a fall-out over whose turn it was with the dolls or the pram she just gave us that look and whoever was in the wrong knew it was aimed at them and they would behave themselves. I remember getting into a lot of bother about our behaviour towards the rag-and-bone man one afternoon. In those days you could sell your old rags and it was a good way of making a penny or two extra. As a result, he was a very familiar figure in the Liberties and one day we saw an opportunity for a bit of fun. We jumped on to his cart when he went into one of the houses and started mocking his slightly lop-sided way of walking. He complained to Mammy and she was furious and we were sent to bed without any tea, having been firmly told it wasn't right to mock those less fortunate than we were; he had not chosen to walk that way.

Chrissie was always over visiting her aunty Mrs Harris and we would play our dolly games to our hearts' content. Most of the time we played with them in the lane, taking turns wheeling them up and down in the pram, clucking at every imagined move they made. 'Isn't she a little dote!' we'd say fondly just as we'd heard the grown-ups do. Sometimes we would fall out though, and Chrissie would rebel and go marching off home. Usually the fall-out only lasted a few minutes but sometimes things got a bit more serious. I was older than her by a few months and that gave me some scope to boss her around, just as my sister bossed me. I told her that I would never ever speak to her again unless she gave me her toothpaste. It was a solid pink block of Gibbs toothpaste and it came in its own little container. You had to wet the toothbrush and run it across the block to get some toothpaste on it. She loved that thing – she carried it with her everywhere – but in the end she gave in. Later that evening I remember my mammy saying, 'Wherever did that toothpaste come from, Kathleen?' And before I could think of a reply, she answered the question herself. 'Kathleen O'Malley, you'll be the death of me. Chrissie Dumphy's mammy is at the door wanting it back!'

One afternoon when I returned to school after the midday meal a nun asked me if I had had my lunch. I told her, 'No, Sister,' because I hadn't had the rice pudding which Mammy always gave us at the end, and which to me completed the meal. Every so often after that day, one of the nuns would ask me precisely what I'd had to eat at lunchtime. Perhaps I unwittingly gave them ammunition against my mother later on when they would accuse her of not being able to look after us properly now that Tommy was gone.

Sarah Louise and I carried on going to school at George's Hill; Mammy did her jobs whenever and wherever she could. Even without Tommy's pay cheque she was managing to get by. But unbeknownst to us, the NSPCC – or the cruelty men as everyone called them locally – had had their eye on her for a while, ever since she left the home for unmarried mothers having given birth to me, in fact. Although they were a charity and were supposed to be on the side of the children, the fact was that wasn't how anyone in the Liberties saw it. We kids were all frightened to death by the very thought of them. Everyone talked about and lived in fear of what the cruelty men did but what my sisters and I didn't know was that we had a lot more to fear than most. People gossiped and said that they split up families or sent children away who were mitching school but what we didn't realise – because we didn't know the word illegitimate at this time – was that the fact that Mammy hadn't been married to either my or my older sister's daddy was the greatest crime of all. Although her brief marriage to Tommy Byrne had temporarily taken her off their immediate radar, now she was a widow all that had changed.

Completely out of the blue we were summoned to attend court even though we had done nothing wrong as far as we could see. It didn't matter to them that we had Irish dancing lessons and a hot meal every day and ribbons in our hair. It didn't matter that we never mitched off school or hung around the pubs asking for pennies as so many of our neighbours' children did. They didn't inspect our house or ask us what we ate or how often we changed our clothes; they simply made a judgement about my mother.

On 3 September 1947, I, along with my elder sister, came

before Justice Fitzpatrick at Metropolitan Children's Court, Dublin Castle. The complainant was Inspector Annie Wogan of the NSPCC, and Sarah Louise and I the defendants. We were charged not with being illegitimate but with being 'destitute'. They didn't specify what they meant by that so my mother had no way of appealing. We had no legal representation and no right of defence even if we could have afforded one. We were not asked anything, nor was my mother. After this nonsense of a 'hearing' a decision was swiftly reached: we should be taken away from our mother and sent to St Vincent's Goldenbridge, a Certified Industrial School, until the eve of our sixteenth birthdays. On the committal form it stated 'stepfather dead' and next to 'grounds for committal' was written 'destitute'. The admission form for Goldenbridge, which I have also seen in recent years, went one step further. State if 'illegitimate' it asks, and the simple reply was inserted: 'yes'.

That my little sister, Lydia, was spared makes a further mockery of the case against us. If we were considered destitute, then she too was destitute, since we all lived under the same roof, in the same circumstances. It certainly wasn't her age because mere babies were taken off their parents by the NSPCC; it could only be because she was born within the sanctity of holy wedlock and so there was hope for the salvation of her soul. My mother never signed anything allowing us to be taken away from her. She wasn't required to. She had committed the gravest sin of all in having two children out of wedlock and they didn't need her permission to do what they wanted. I was too young to understand what happened. I had no idea what the word destitute meant or how it applied to us, but I knew that Mammy was more upset than I had ever seen her and that nothing any of us could do seemed to cheer her up. I know we went home after the court and started to prepare what we needed for our going away. But I knew I didn't want to go and Mammy didn't want us to either, so why was it happening? I certainly had heard about the cruelty men before – Mrs Harris was always threatening her children with them if they didn't behave – but I never expected them to have anything to do with us. But why now? The world was suddenly a much more confusing place than I had previously imagined.

My world was falling apart but I didn't know why. I just wanted it to stop. I was sitting on the edge of the bed and Mammy was putting on my shoes only she couldn't tie the laces because her hands were shaking. She was trying to explain to me that I was going away for a while, to a nice school with the nuns, where they would look after me, it was for my own good. It would help me. I remember she was doing up my shoes and wouldn't look at me and I started to feel a horrible hurting feeling inside. All I could hear was 'for your own good', 'going away', '*away*', and I wanted to hurt her back so I said, 'You're not my real mammy anyway. My real mammy is away and she's going to come back and take me away from you.' She didn't look up, she just kept on saying, 'You and Sarah Louise are going away to a nice place called Goldenbridge. It won't be for long.'

Chapter 5

I had come from the slums of Dublin, from a tenement building right in the heart of the over-crowded, polluted city centre, but nothing would compare with the feeling of dread I experienced when I first saw St Vincent's Industrial School, or Goldenbridge, as it was known. It was a huge, forbidding building, which hid its ugliness behind a high grey wall. It had large windows and inside it had dark, echoey rooms. I had never seen a prison before but, in my mind's eye, this was what I had imagined it would look like.

One of the nuns opened the door and marched us through up to the orphanage. We did not see any other part of the school as we were going to be kept separate. Our classrooms were bare. There were no books on the shelves or pictures on the walls. There was just row upon row of desks which didn't match. This, the nun said, was where we would come each day to do our lessons. There were forty or so in each class and we were divided up according to our respective ages. Sarah Louise and I would be in different classes.

Then we were taken to the dormitories where we would sleep

at night. These were two huge, cold rooms with beds lined up top-to-tail with the foot of one almost touching the head of the other, and so on down the dormitory. There was just enough room to pass between each bed. Having given me and my sister beds as far apart from each other as possible, the nun disappeared off down the echoey corridor. I wanted to cry; I had been holding the feelings in for so long my throat ached and my lip was sore from biting it. I longed for Sarah Louise to say something cheeky under her breath but she didn't, she didn't say anything, she just stared out of the window as though I wasn't there.

I listened to the nun's footsteps disappearing off and the sound of her habit swish, swish, swishing on the wooden floor. It seemed to echo for a very long time. I wanted to cry but I didn't because Mammy wasn't there to comfort me. I sat on the little hard bed and tried not to think how long I was going to have to spend there.

The next day we were woken up by a loud bell when it was still dark and I scrambled out of bed and tried to copy what the rest of the girls did. We said our prayers, we got dressed underneath our nightdresses and still no one said anything or told me what was happening. All I can remember from this time onwards was a terrible sense of fear about what had happened to Mammy. I kept wondering where she was – maybe she'd been locked up too? Was that why we couldn't go home to our own beds any more? I was five years old and very frightened.

The food was horrible. There was tea and a slice of white bread and dripping at breakfast; a plate of thin stew in the middle of the day; a piece of bread after school, until supper, when you had bread and dripping. And you had to be quick with the bread: if you didn't snatch a piece the minute it arrived, you would find that it had all gone and you would have nothing to eat from lunchtime till the next morning. I hated the food from the first day to the last but my tummy was empty and rumbling the whole time so I ate it and didn't complain. I tried not to think of the lovely food Mammy made at home and just got on with it. We were given a plate and mug, made of enamel to prevent breakages, but even they were chipped and rough from years and years of hard use.

The food never changed except at the weekends. On Sundays we had a sausage which was very different from the ones we used to have at home. These were full of fat and hard to chew and sat on top of a little mound of lumpy, watery mashed potato. If you were lucky you got carrots but usually it was accompanied by a pile of watery-coloured cabbage complete with slugs which no one had bothered to wash out. And I was always thirsty but we were never allowed to get ourselves even a drink of water; the kitchen was completely out of bounds during the day. But then I saw what the other girls did and even though I was worried it might not be very clean, I started to copy them. When they went to the loo they drank the water as it flushed out of the cistern into the toilet. If you cupped your hands tightly together you could get just enough to quench your thirst.

The toilet facilities were worse. The greatest shock at Goldenbridge, the thing that would have shamed every family in our lane, was that there was no toilet paper; it simply wasn't provided. The walls were our toilet paper. We wiped our bottoms with our fingers, then we wiped them, in turn, on the walls. It was so disgusting: long brown stains were left all the way up the wall and the smell was enough to make your stomach turn. The first day I went in there I assumed that the paper had just run out and this was what the girls had done in a crisis. But it wasn't a one-off, it was a regular occurrence. The toilets would get blocked and one of the girls would have to clear the blockage with nothing but a bucket of water and an old cloth. There was always a lingering stench.

Regularly each week the nuns would humiliate us. We would gather in the big yard and remove our pants. We would then, each in turn, put them up on a pole and the other children would have to raise their hands to vote on whether the pants were soiled or not. Those unfortunate girls who had dirty pants were beaten there and then, in front of everybody. Then the pants were taken down off the pole to go to the laundry. I never did understand it. How could we be expected to keep ourselves totally clean?

I don't remember ever learning anything at that school. We sat at our school desks every day but the nuns didn't even have lessons prepared for us. Nobody seemed to expect us to be able to do anything and in time we didn't. We sat with our books open and stared vacantly out of the window. One day just blurred into the next.

Every afternoon we went to work making rosary beads in the workshop. One of the nuns told me that the school was famous for making the beads and we all were expected to get involved, even those as young as four. We were told that it was a great honour and we little girls were going to make the individual sections for the Hail Marys. We were given a box of short, fine wires which had been cut to a special size by the older girls. We were shown how to make the male hook at the end of the wire and then thread on to it ten beads of the same size and colour before making the female hook at the end to keep them in place. The nuns said that keen eyesight, nimble fingers and small hands were perfect for the work, but we must concentrate; talking or whispering were absolutely forbidden. I looked around me; everyone seemed to know exactly what they were doing. There were children of all ages, threading the little beads on as fast as they could, never looking up from their work. Soon I became just like them. From Monday to Friday, we started work at four in the afternoon and it didn't matter how long it took, we stayed there until we had finished the required number of beads, even if it meant not having tea until late. On Saturday we did a half day.

The beads came in all sorts of pretty colours but any temptation to turn the task into fun was quickly driven out of us. The nun in charge told us that we had to make sixty decads each afternoon after school and more at the weekend when we worked all morning. If we didn't make enough we would be punished. You couldn't rush it; if you tried to get it over with more quickly you just ended up cutting your fingers. After my first week I decided that although rosaries might look nice, making the beads was a horrible job: the wire was very thin and because it sat for hours on end on the first joint of the left index finger, it soon started cutting into your skin. There was nothing you could do to prevent it and before too long, the wire would be resting on an open wound. My hands became red raw, blisters developed and blood flowed from our fingertips as the wire cut into us repeatedly. But there was never any let up for injury, there was no point in crying because no one would listen and there was certainly never any question of stopping. The whole operation was supervised constantly by three or four nuns who never took their eyes off what we were doing.

The nuns paced up and down between the rows of work benches and if they were not happy with what they saw, they would simply throw the decads back at us. One time I got the colours a bit jumbled up and one of the nuns hit me on the hand with her pointy stick. 'That's all wrong, you clumsy girl. Do them again.' I feared her wrath so much I sat there trembling afterwards, then I unthreaded them and started all over again. At first I hated the silence at Goldenbridge, particularly when making the beads. But something about the work, day in and day out, stopped me even wanting to talk and after a while just doing it made me feel subdued.

Throughout our days at the school we lived in fear of making the nuns angry and receiving a beating. You could be beaten for anything and everything; there did not have to be a reason. Most of the nuns carried with them a thick length of wood called a slapper which they used to beat us on the fronts and backs of our hands. It was standard to have to stand and receive six or twelve lashes of the slapper and it hurt so much you had to bite your lip to stop yourself from crying out with the pain.

One day a whisper went round that Santa Claus made a special visit to the school at Christmas. I could hardly believe my ears but it was the older girls who whispered it, they said it happened every year. I hadn't been there very long but I knew better than to show how excited I was feeling; on the inside, though, I could hardly hold it in – it seemed too good to be true. Suddenly Santa Claus appeared in his bright red suit and snowy white beard. A huge wicker basket simultaneously appeared from nowhere, crammed full of brightly coloured parcels. It was magical, incredible, it made me feel dizzy just seeing it all. I had seen Santa before with Mammy and my sisters and like the other little girls could hardly contain my excitement.

'Now children,' began Santa cheerfully, 'I am going to reach into the basket, pull out a parcel and, with the help of this kind Sister, I am going to call out the name that is written on it. When you hear your name, you should raise your hand and the parcel will be handed to you. Is that clear, children?'

'Yes!' we all chorused, not wanting to sound to enthusiastic or greedy.

And so he began. I hardly dared hope that there would be something for me among the presents and I waited and waited as he reeled through the long list of names and suddenly my sister's name was called, and then it was me – Kathleen O'Malley – and I jumped up to receive my present. I sat there holding it so carefully until the last parcel had been distributed, and then – joy of joys – we were finally allowed to tear off the shiny wrappings and see what was inside. Jigsaw puzzles, spinning tops, teddy bears all fell out of the wrapping paper to shouts of delight. My gift was a doll. She was a lovely little pink thing with lots of blonde curls. It was just what I wanted. I was hugging her when one of the big girls appeared, snatched the doll and the wrapping paper from my hands and before I could object, had whisked them both off. I started to shout after her and promptly burst into tears. She was halfway across the room by this time but came back, and standing over me, looking down at me, said harshly, 'Don't be an eejit! It's not yours to keep.' I cried even more. No wonder it seemed too good to be true – *it was too good to be true*. I hadn't understood it at all. Santa's toys were just there for show. They were for the local people to see what the nuns were doing for the poor children. They weren't for us at all. The toys went back into the cupboard again to be parcelled up and stored away until the following year, when I would doubtless receive the same doll again for five minutes.

As 1947 came to a close I began to think that we would be in Goldenbridge for ever. We had been there since September and yet the difference between then and now was vast. I didn't notice the physical changes in myself because we didn't have mirrors, but in my older sister, whom I had always looked up to, the changes were very noticeable. She had always been so pretty, so confident and yet, even in this short time, she seemed like a totally different person. I rarely spoke to her because the nuns made sure we were kept apart wherever possible. We were in separate classrooms; we had different tasks to complete after schoo.; we never ate at the same table at mealtimes. Although Mammy had always said we were as different as chalk and cheese, she was my big sister, I still had her high up there on a pedestal and I longed for her approval as much as ever. More than that, I just felt so far away from home and she was my one link with what had gone before. I missed Sarah Louise very much, but the nuns made it clear that any closeness between us girls, sisters or otherwise, was to be totally discouraged.

When we passed in the refectory or the dormitory she looked at me blankly almost without recognition. I'd begun to think she'd forgotten who I was and I felt more lonely and miserable than I ever had in my entire life. My sixth birthday came and went at the end of March and no one even mentioned it. I tried not to think about being with Mammy and putting the jellies on the window ledge and choosing the icing colour on the cake but it was hard and made me long to be back home again. I tried not to remember my old life, I just willed the days of my new life to pass without beatings or disgrace or tears.

At Easter we got an egg. Not a chocolate one decorated with a chicken made out of frosted icing on it, like we used to when we were at home, but a whole hardboiled egg. Still, an egg was very unusual and it was quite a treat for us. The nuns just handed them to us in a totally blank manner, with no indication that this was something to enjoy and to savour. They seemed to be determined never to allow us any excitement in our lives; the more pleased we looked, the more they frowned. One of the girls who had been there ever since she was a baby later told me that this egg was a once a year treat and it was always administered in the same mean way.

In the new year, about six months into our detention at Goldenbridge, I was walking past my sister in the corridor when she caught my eye and put out a hand to stop me. No one was near us and she whispered to me under her breath, 'We've got to get out!'

I just said, 'Yes', hardly able to believe my ears that the old Sarah Louise was still there after all.

She said we had to wait for the right time. If we got it wrong the *gardai* would come for us. She said it all with great seriousness and although I felt a bit frightened of what would happen to us if the police caught us, all I could think about was the possibility that we might soon be home again and it seemed worth it whatever the risks. But months passed and although my sister never said anything directly again, I could see by her eyes that the plan was still on: she was as desperate to get out as I was.

In August 1948 we escaped. It's odd that despite the fact that I can recall that planning conversation as clearly as if it were yesterday, I don't remember exactly how we got out. Perhaps we scaled the five-foot-high perimeter wall or perhaps we darted out of the back gate when it was briefly opened. Either way, we ended up by the canal which ran along the back of the school and just set off running as fast as our legs could carry us. We didn't know what direction Dublin was, all we knew was that the canal led to the Liffey and we lived near there. All we could think about was getting as far away as possible from that dreaded grey wall and our torturers. We had not thought of the likely consequences of our action, of what the nuns would do to us if they caught us; we just could not get home fast enough. All we wanted was to see Mammy again.

After a while a Guinness cart appeared and my sister saw our chance. Those huge shire horses pulling the cart laden down with Guinness barrels was such a welcome sight, so familiar from our old life, and it was bound to be going into the city centre because they all did. Anyway we had no other choice. We had no money and the idea of walking five or six miles was very daunting. When it came past we grabbed on to the back, holding on by our fingers with the full weight of our bodies dangling down and underneath the cart. It was just like the game we used to play only this time it was for real. The drayman was familiar with street kids because he flicked his whip over the back of the cart from time to time but somehow we managed to dodge it and stayed on until our hands were so sore from holding on, I was sure I couldn't last a minute longer. Sarah Louise shouted above the din of the cart that she'd seen a place she recognized and we jumped off and ducked down an alleyway out of sight.

We ran all the way home. I can remember as clearly as though it was yesterday, pushing open the old red front door of number twenty-nine and leaping up the stairs and banging on our door, breathlessly waiting to see Mammy's surprised face. We knocked and knocked and no one came. We banged louder until eventually Mrs Harris, our neighbour across the landing, poked her head around the door. She looked completely stunned to see us.

'Whatever are you two doing here?' she asked as though she had seen a pair of ghosts.

'Where's our mammy?' asked Sarah Louise.

'She's gone to Goldenbridge to visit you, as it happens,' replied our neighbour, looking at us suspiciously.

We waited on the step until eventually Mammy arrived home. She came up the steps with Lydia in her arms and she started to ask us what we were doing and how we'd got there, but then she just seemed to change her mind and her eyes welled up with tears and she put my baby sister down and held her arms out to us. We clutched tightly to each other, she kissed our faces and it seemed as though we would never let each other go. We had been away from each other for nearly a year and we hugged and hugged, with little Lydia in the middle of it all, as though we could somehow make up for all that lost time.

Eventually, she managed to pull herself away and step back. She looked at us properly and asked what all the bruises and red marks on our skin were. We said we didn't know. We didn't want her to start crying again. She asked us why we were both scratching our heads constantly. What was wrong with us? But then she was crying again over and over. I had never seen her so upset before. She kept saying that the nuns had treated us very badly and had made us ill. We would not be punished for running away because we were never going to go back there. She would fight whoever necessary to ensure that we did not have to.

In the meantime she got the fire going and asked Mrs Harris to pop down to the shop for us to get some bacon as a special treat for our tea. She boiled up about ten kettles of water and made the biggest bath we had ever seen. She tried not to stare at us when we took off our ragged clothes but she told me later, when we were well again, that our ribs were sticking out, we had the red marks of scabies and ringworm all over our bodies, and she had never seen so many head lice in all her born days. She cleaned us gently and wrapped us in the lovely warm blankets from the bed whilst we had our tea. She put ointment on our skin and combed our hair as gently as she could.

When the *gardai* came banging on our door later that night to find out if we'd run back home Mammy was ready for them. She told them that there was no way anyone was taking us off her again. She had seen the state we came home in and we'd been neglected very badly. We were malnourished and ill and if we were to be taken off her again it would be over her dead body.

Mammy was as good as her word, she went back to court and this time she won. She wasn't daunted by the officialdom and the way they patronised her. She had seen how they looked after her children and she was convinced they didn't have a leg to stand on. I've no idea how she did it, but on 17 August 1948, she got our committal overturned, which was a very rare thing. The reasons had to be overwhelming. Perhaps if a single mother had got married during the time her children were in an Industrial School the Department of Education might look more kindly on a request to overturn the committal, but even marriage did not provide automatic grounds for reversing the decision. If a parent had remained unmarried, it didn't matter what she wanted or thought, and it didn't matter what her financial circumstances were, her child would not be returned to her. That simply did not happen. Given that my mother had not married I can only think it was overturned on the grounds of health. But no reason was ever given and the scant piece of paper she was given simply said: 'Discharge approved'.

Chapter 6

Lydia had been just a toddler when we left and now she was a noisy, adventurous child of three and a bit years old. She had changed so much whilst we were away and, though I didn't show it, I couldn't help but envy her that year she'd had on her own with Mammy. She was too young to know anything of where we had been, and since Sarah Louise and I never spoke of it, we were all three of us a bit like strangers and very cautious of one another. But gradually things returned to normal and in due course we picked up on our old life almost as though there had been no interruption. When the new school year started, we returned to George's Hill and Goldenbridge began to seem like a dim and distant nightmare.

Just as my sister had done at the same point, at the age of seven I prepared to make my Holy Communion. We had been learning the catechism for months with extra lessons after school and at the weekends to make sure that we understood what Holy Communion was about. It was a large class with many of the local children in attendance. The words sin, guilt, shame, repentance and forgiveness had been drummed in to us repeatedly.

The nuns kept repeating to us that we had reached the 'age of reason' and could tell right from wrong; it was a very important undertaking and our time had come. We were told that we would be taking the body of Christ in the form of a thin white wafer and we must never let this 'body' touch our teeth. This was a mortal sin and you'd burn in hell if you did so.

The highlight of all this extra work was that Mammy took me on a special shopping trip. We bought a short white dress, a veil, hornpipe shoes, which were patent, with a chrome buckle on the front, and little white ankle socks. Normally any one of these would have been highly exciting but on this occasion they paled into insignificance next to the brown coat complete with a velvet collar which Mammy insisted on. I remember her telling the shop assistant very proudly that I was about to make my Holy Communion and the coat had to be of the best quality, she wanted me to have a velvet collar as I had very sensitive skin.

The night before the ceremony 29 Lower Bridge Street was devoted to preparation. I had my bath in front of the fire, washed my hair and Mammy curled it in strips of rag she had torn up. I then had to go to bed for what proved a very uncomfortable night's sleep, but it was worth it for when I woke and the rags were removed my hair was a mass of ringlets, just as she had said it would be. I got dressed in my finery, my black patent hornpipe shoes, and best of all, my new soft chocolate-brown and white checked coat.

Mammy walked with me to George's Hill and along the way people stopped and commented on me in my little white veil, all spruced up and holy-looking, and some of them even gave me a farthing or a ha'penny which Mammy let me keep as it was the day of my Holy Communion. I asked Mammy to look after my money since I had already decided that I would put them in my Post Office savings to save it for a rainy day. She escorted me, proud as punch, to the gates of the convent and there she left me; parents weren't allowed into the service itself.

Along with eighty-three other children I took my first Holy Communion. It took a long time to get through it because there were so many of us, but I sat stiff as a statue until it came to my turn and then I got up and received the body of Christ. I took it all very seriously. Afterwards we had breakfast in the nuns' refectory which was such a treat. I held the nuns at George's Hill in awe, I desperately wanted to be like them and this seemed like a positive step in the right direction. The whole event was quite overwhelming. Being in the convent itself, let alone eating a meal at the table which the holy nuns used, was almost as much of a treat as the lovely brown coat which smelt so new and just like the shop. I drank it all in.

The summer after our release we went back to our seaside outings. I loved those days out all the more now I knew what it was like to be locked away in damp rooms all day and never see the sunlight. It was during one of those trips that Mammy met a man called Paddy McNamara.

Paddy started chatting to Mammy one day on the beach at Dollymount. Sarah Louise and I were playing a bit further off with our friends and couldn't believe our eyes. He was older than Mammy but very handsome and neatly turned out. Mammy had not been her old happy-go-lucky self for so long that we were just pleased to see her smiling at him and not getting up to move away. He made her laugh like she did in the old days and it was music to our ears.

Mammy didn't say anything about him on the way home but the next Sunday she didn't even suggest the alternative beach at Malahide as she normally would, she just announced we were going back to Dollymount as we'd had such fun the previous weekend. And would you believe who was there when we went back again but the same good-looking man as the previous week, only this time he had his friend with him!

Mammy pretended to be very surprised and even blushed a little when she saw him. This time he chatted to us too and then he and his friend got a great game going which involved swinging us round and round before launching us off into the breaking waves. I was screaming and shouting and enjoying it and Mammy tried to put a stop to it by saying, 'Please, Paddy, would you put Kathleen down, she's frightened. Listen to her, she's terrified.'

He stood up to her and just said, 'She's having a great time, May, she loves it really.' But he stopped because she asked him and smiled at her in that way he had. Looking back it's obvious that this was Paddy McNamara's way of courting my mother, flirting with her and playing boisterous games with us. She fell for it: he seemed like a nice family man and before the year was out, he was permanently in our lives.

Mammy told us that Paddy had a family of his own but his wife had sadly died and his two children, a boy and a girl, were being looked after by his mother. So he was a family man in some ways, only, like a lot of Irishmen in the fifties who found themselves in the same situation, he wasn't actually raising them, someone else was doing that for him. He didn't talk about his own family very much and Mammy always frowned if we started asking him what she called impertinent questions. He was a coachbuilder for C.I.E. in Inchicore in Dublin and a very skilled craftsman. Very early on in their courtship he made Mammy a beautiful new wardrobe out of polished mahogany or walnut; it was a work of art Mammy said and the nicest thing anyone had ever given her. He came over to us about once a week or so. Some times he'd bring round a bit of stewing steak or something special like that and Mammy would fry up the onions and make a lovely stew for us all. The delicious savoury smell would fill up the two rooms, and Mammy would chat and joke to him as she cooked. And we liked those evenings too; it was different having a man around but we didn't object to him because he always brought us sweets.

One of Mammy's main jobs at this time was at St Thomas's Hospital where she worked every day. I really liked the hospital – I liked the hustle and bustle and seeing the nurses in their uniforms coming and going looking important. One day I'd had to come back from school early for some reason and I was making my way to meet Mammy at the hospital. Our neighbour Luke McCabe, who worked as a porter at the covered market opposite George's Hill, offered me a ride on his handcart. He lifted me on to the handcart so I was facing him. Then he put his hand up my dress and said it was to steady me and stop me from falling. He moved his hand up further, just inside my knickers, and kept it there. It didn't feel right to me but I didn't think too much of it and I didn't want to make a fuss – he was our neighbour and he was giving me a lift to my mammy. When we stopped outside the hospital I saw a group of young men just looking at us and they seemed to stop talking before they moved off.

McCabe then said, 'Put your hand in my pocket, there's something in there for you.' So I put my hand in his pocket but I didn't find any money, I just felt something hard and he said, 'Can you feel that?' and I said, 'Yes.' Then I ran off to meet Mammy as fast as I could.

I didn't tell Mammy what had happened or anything about getting a ride because she'd been feeling a bit poorly recently and I hadn't wanted to worry her. I decided to keep what had happened on the cart to myself. I tried to avoid Luke McCabe after that but he acted as though nothing wrong had happened and would always ask for me rather than any of the other kids to run messages for him for a ha'penny or a farthing. Mammy never asked who the money came from. All the kids ran messages for the neighbours.

*   *   *

Mammy hadn't been able to do her cleaning jobs for a while because she'd come home one day with a new baby brother for us, Paul. We were a bit surprised, but once we'd got over the shock, were as pleased as punch to have a real live baby to play with, to rock in our arms and say, 'Isn't he a little dote now,' and all the things we'd pretended to do with our plastic dolls. We didn't know anything about how these things happened but we were just so pleased that Mammy wasn't feeling poorly any more and was more like her old self again.

One day when we were all at home, I was playing with my dolls and pram, Mammy was knitting by the fire, I heard Mr McCabe call out for one of the local boys, Francine Byrne, to go and fetch him some water from the tap. Francie was a little boy who lived nearby and who spent a lot of time at his granny's just down the lane. He was always hanging around, running errands for people, much as I and several other children did. I heard his name called again and again and still there was no answer so I asked Mammy if it was OK for me to go.

I knocked on Mr McCabe's door, collected the empty kettle, queued by the tap for him and when it was my turn filled it up. I took it back to the door of his house and he told me to come inside, he was in the back room. The McCabes had two rooms exactly the same as ours; his sister-in-law slept in the front room, he and his wife Georgina slept in the back. As soon as I went in there, he bolted the door and grabbed me roughly round the waist. Still holding me firmly he sat down on the settee and then pulled me on to his lap and put my legs on either side of his so that I was straddling him. I started to cry; he was breathing deeply and I didn't understand what was happening. 'Leave me alone,' I said but he just carried on.

He said, 'I'll leave you alone in a few minutes,' barely looking up at me. He was wearing a long dark coat that was unbuttoned and I saw him reach down and open his trousers. Suddenly he was hurting me. I didn't know why he was trying to do that, only that there was a ripping pain through my body and I wanted it to stop. He kept pushing and hurting me with his rocking and moving.

Suddenly the moving stopped and he started fumbling about. I burst into tears and he told me not to be such a baby. Still sobbing I said, 'I'm going to tell Georgina.'

He gripped my arm and said, 'If you tell Georgina she'll have you put away.' He didn't need to say any more. He knew that I had been taken away before; he knew that I knew what the cruelty men could do. It was the worst threat he could have come up with and he knew it would ensure my silence. He unbolted his door and let me out.

That night I became ill. I started to run a temperature and at midnight, Mammy gave me a glass of hot milk and a tablet. The following morning I was worse, I had dark circles around my eyes and was very pale, so she tried to keep me off school. But I didn't want to stay at home. I told her I didn't want to miss any days as the school term was about to end. I kept thinking about the cruelty men coming to get me for what I had done and that *he* was downstairs. When I came home for lunch she tried again to keep me there but I just would not stay.

Three days later, with me getting worse by the day, she took me to Lord Edward Street Children's Hospital, and reported that I wasn't very well. They gave me a cursory examination to check for fever, declared there was nothing wrong with me and sent me home. That night I hadn't improved and so she gave me another tablet to wash down with a glass of hot milk. The following day when I came home for lunch, Mammy was determined to get to the bottom of it – as if her mother's instinct knew something was badly wrong. She said, 'What's the matter with you, Kathleen?' I was walking with difficulty, bent over and hunched up.

'Oh, I've scalded myself,' I said. She told me to lie down on the bed so that she could take a look at me. Then she pulled up my dress. I couldn't see what she could but I knew it was something terrible.

'Who did this to you?' she demanded, her voice rising.

'Nobody, Mammy. I've just scalded myself.'

'Tell me who did this to you,' she shouted.

'Oh, you'll murder me, Mammy, if I tell you.'

'I won't murder you,' she said in a slow and deliberate voice, 'but I'll murder whoever did this to you.'

'It was Lukey McCabe.'

'I'll kill him,' she shouted.

'Don't go near him,' I cried. 'Please don't go near him.'

I was terrified he'd have me sent away to a school and would do bad things to her but Mammy wasn't listening any more. She rushed out, went across the landing and then came back with Mrs Harris and showed her the state I was in. Then they went into the other room so I couldn't quite hear their conversation, except from time to time, the name McCabe filtered through, and Mrs Harris said, 'Keep your voice down.' Then she came and took my knickers and offered to wash them for Mammy.

Mammy said that we were going to have to go to the general hospital, St Stephen's. Somehow we got there – she carried me some of the way and the rest I walked, leaning on her when we went up the hill. We went into the main part of the hospital and suddenly there were a whole crowd of people who wanted to have a look at me. There was a Dr Patrick O'Sullivan, a Dr Francis Bourke and various others who got involved. I later found out that when Dr O'Sullivan tried to examine my genitals he found it almost impossible. They were so red, swollen and tender that he could only conduct an examination of the external area. Any time he tried to get me to open my legs fully I screamed out in agony. He did at least see that I had quite a lot of discharge and he noted this down as well as the numerous scratches and bruises on my body, which further confirmed my story that I had been attacked by someone much larger and stronger than I was. Mammy made me repeat what I had said to her again, that my neighbour had done it to me and, yes, she did want to press charges, so a couple of police officers were called in to take a statement.

Just as I felt the ordeal couldn't get any worse, the doctor announced that a vaginal smear needed to be taken to give to the police as evidence. There was more poking about in my privates and then a dull pain as samples were taken and at last it was all finished with and Mammy and I and Mrs Harris were allowed to go and rest in the waiting room. After half an hour, during which nobody said a word, Mammy just squeezed my hand from time to time and cuddled me, the doctor came back to us looking very grave. For a minute I thought he was bracing himself to tell me that I was going to die so I was almost relieved when he explained that he thought that I had contracted gonorrhoea. I didn't know what that strange-sounding word beginning with 'g' meant but I could see from Mammy's and Mrs Harris's faces that it was very serious.

Eventually we were allowed to go home. We picked up my sisters from our neighbour who had been keeping an eye on them. Mammy just told them I wasn't feeling very well and I would have to go to the hospital every day to be treated. They were nice to me and Sarah Louise even said I could have all the next turns on the roller skates when I was feeling better.

The next day Mammy said again she was going to press charges against the man who had done this to me. That afternoon she took me to the home of the police doctor, Francis Bourke. When we arrived Garda Friel from the local police station was already there waiting. Once again I had to go through the horrible, degrading ordeal of an internal examination. Although I was allowed to keep my vest on, I cried when the doctor examined me. It was difficult because I was very sore still and upset, but Dr Bourke managed to take a smear and he gave it to the *garda* who was waiting in the next room.

The policeman accompanied us back home, because he now had the task of summoning McCabe and taking him to see Dr Bourke for a similar examination. I heard Mammy say to Mrs Harris that he must be even more simple than she'd thought he was because he apparently went willingly, offering no objections. But perhaps no one explained to him what was going on. I can only assume (with hindsight) that he had not been told that I had been infected with gonorrhoea. He must have been fairly confident that they would not be able to prove the word of an eight-year-old against his own. Anyway, he was examined and the two envelopes containing my own smear and his one were then taken down to the police station.

Mammy told me that the *garda* had taken Luke McCabe away to the police station in Kevin Street where Inspector Thomas Lynch charged him. They took a statement from him and he just said, 'I swear to God Almighty that I'm innocent. I've done none of this. I am innocent of the whole lot of it. I want to see my solicitor.' Then bail was set at one hundred pounds for him, and his father and brother had to pledge fifty pounds each. This sum was pronounced too little for such a serious offence by Judge McCarthy at a later date and it was increased to three hundred for him and one hundred pounds each for his father and brother.

More than fifty years on, I've had plenty of time to think about my attacker's apparent confidence. He must have had every reason to think that he was completely untouchable. He was married, he had a job that earned him three pounds a week and a wife who also worked. And child rape – what was that? In 1950 such an accusation was almost unheard of. Furthermore for such charges to be made by a poor single mother with illegitimate children – who would listen to such a person? Yet despite all this, on 17 July, he was sent on remand to Mountjoy prison in Dublin.

On the same day, two full days after the samples were taken, Garda Friel handed over the two envelopes containing my and McCabe's smears to the State pathologist, Dr McGrath of University College Dublin. His job was to analyse them and reach a conclusion as to what infection, if any, they presented. His findings were to play a central role in the future trial. The fact that they had also remained in a locker for two full days would also prove to be critical. The next day Garda Friel collected from us the knickers that Mrs Harris had so helpfully washed. These would also be used as an exhibit at the trial.

The trial date was provisionally set for 10 October and Mammy told me that I would be asked to stand up and speak and that I did not need to be frightened, but I did need to tell everyone what McCabe had done to me. She didn't say any more about what would happen if I did, she just told me the facts and that we should try to get back to living our normal everyday life.

I had to receive penicillin every two hours for a period of time, so we went back and forth to the hospital repeatedly on foot. Apparently they tried to get me to stay at the hospital and offered me a bed but I was so traumatised and distressed I refused to be separated from Mammy for even five minutes. As it was it felt as though I lived at the hospital. My two sisters continued to be very sweet and concerned about my tummy bug and lent me their toys to play with. I was scared that if they knew the truth they would tell and I lived in fear that somehow they would find out. In total my treatment lasted for six weeks, though Dr O'Sullivan said I'd been lucky because they'd got it early and had managed to get it under control quickly. I was so grateful to the doctor for making the pain go away, I asked Mammy if we could buy him a present for being so nice to me. We had very little money at this time because Mammy couldn't do her cleaning jobs, but she bought him a luxury selection box of chocolates with a big bow on the outside, just to make me happy.

Luke McCabe was on remand for a week, then granted bail and allowed home and we had to carry on living in close proximity to him. Every day my mother had to pass his door or cross him in the lane. Every night she went to bed knowing that the man who had interfered with her daughter was sleeping immediately below her. She was full of impotent rage because there was nothing she could do or say. Sexual abuse was not something people were prepared to discuss in god-fearing, Holy Ireland; shameful things like that just weren't supposed to happen, but the shadow of it had come into our street and hung over our two rooms. The neighbours turned against her and there were no comforting words of support or offers of cups of tea. They didn't approve of her making such a disgraceful incident public – it would have been better to sweep it all under the carpet. It seemed that no matter how awful the crime, you didn't involve the *gardaí*.

Much as she was hurt by the neighbours' coldness towards her, my mother was determined that McCabe was not going to be allowed to get away with his crime. The more he noisily protested his innocence to anyone who would listen, the more she felt herself being ostracised by the tight-knit community of Lower Bridge Street.

One day, however, in a very minor way, she got her own back. It was early in the morning, we were upstairs in our rooms and she heard his repugnant voice outside in the lane and she just couldn't stand it any more. She took the bucket that we used for the toilet at night and emptied the entire contents straight out of the window directly over his head. He was soaked and indignant and although it was quite clear whose window it had come out of, he couldn't prove it. We couldn't believe what she had done. I was glad that he had been humiliated, no matter in how small a way. It was hardly an adequate revenge but it was something.

On 8 August 1950 at Dublin District Court the first of several court hearings for me and McCabe was held. Certain key facts were established. I recall very little about the occasion, though I do remember having to point at McCabe to confirm his identity, which was a quite terrifying thing to have to do in front of a sea of stern adult faces, some of whom were wearing strange wigs and long dark gowns. I gave an account of what took place between 10 and 14 July when my mother discovered my illness and took me to St Stephen's. It was all written up by the court stenographer.

The doctors from St Stephen's testified as did Garda Friel and the state pathologist Dr McGrath. He had analysed both the smears which he had drawn conclusions about and the washed knickers which unsurprisingly showed 'no signs of seminal stains'. The two envelopes containing the smears were called exhibit one and exhibit two and were handed over for presentation at the eventual trial. Neither my mother nor McCabe was asked to give a statement.

The 10 October trial date was postponed. On 25 October I made a second court appearance. This time Mammy's statement about what happened during those few days in July was also written up, as were the statements of our neighbour Mary Harris, Inspector Lynch from Kevin Street police station and Dr Francis Bourke who had taken the smears on 15 July. Mr McCabe was also present but was not required to speak. He was, however, bailed for a second time for one hundred pounds and his father and brother also had to post bail for fifty pounds each. So he had to find a total sum of two hundred pounds to stay out of jail, a not inconsiderable sum for a grocer's porter living in the tenements of Dublin. But McCabe had no intention of going to jail and made sure he found the money to keep his freedom.

The whole affair was very confusing. So much time had passed since McCabe locked me in his room and assaulted me. Sometimes it was difficult to remember everything. Mammy said the same. After the initial report to the police, they didn't ask her any questions again about how I got ill, or on what day she noticed I was walking funny or anything for over three months. Meanwhile Mammy did her best to keep things normal and only she and I knew that the trial was looming. We went to school, had our buns and cocoa at the Iveagh, even kept up our dancing lessons, but what we didn't know was that a menace far, far worse than our neighbour was lurking in the background.

From the moment I had told Mammy about Luke McCabe and the police got involved, the NSPCC had been picking up signals on their radar and, like hawks stalking their prey they were circling ready to dive. As far as the State was concerned, Mammy was an easy target. There she was with a newborn baby, her third born outside of wedlock, and a young daughter who had been raped, or so it was alleged, by a neighbour living in the same building. Clearly these children needed some protection. Completely independently of the trial of Luke McCabe they started proceedings to have all three of us girls committed once more to an Industrial School.

The dawn raid happened on the morning of 22 November 1950, we awoke, petrified, to loud hammering on our door as though someone wanted to break it down. Mammy opened it up dressed only in her nightdress, saw who it was and tried to shut the door but she couldn't. The NSPCC Inspector burst in accompanied by a policeman. We were ordered to get dressed quickly and Mammy was told to gather her things together. Within minutes of their arrival we were being frogmarched out of the building and down to the Metropolitan Children's Court, Dublin Castle. Baby Paul was left with a neighbour.

After a long wait, we were summoned before Judge McCarthy. Once again the complainant was Inspector Wogan and we three girls were the defendants. The charge against us was that we were 'found having a parent who does not exercise proper guardianship'. For our own good it was judged that we would be better off sent as far away as possible from her. Sarah Louise, Lydia and I sat on a bench not really understanding what was going on at all. And then we heard something which did get through. We were going to be sent provisionally to St Vincent's School, Goldenbridge, and should return to the court in two weeks. We would not be allowed home again. Mammy just looked on helplessly as we were led out of the court.

We were in a living nightmare. We were loaded into the back of a police car that was going to take us back to the worst place in the world, the prison from which we had escaped. And this time we had another little prisoner in tow – our five-year-old sister Lydia.

Goldenbridge had scarcely changed since our last visit and seeing it again sent a wave of horror through me. I had done everything I could to forget about it since I was last there, but the instant we were back on the forecourt looking up at those dark, cell-like windows it all came back to me. I was three years older now and it seemed even bleaker than I remembered. Worse, what went on behind those grey walls wasn't a mystery to me this time around. As we entered I overheard one of the nuns say with smug satisfaction, 'Look, we've got the O'Malleys back.'

Of course Lydia found it hardest to adapt to the new regime. She had literally been plucked from her warm bed one morning and ended the day scared and homesick in a huge, draughty dormitory, along with row upon row of other girls, all shivering with cold and hunger. She was very petite and fragile and right from the start she became a target for the bullies. Sarah Louise once came upon one of the older girls swinging Lydia around by her hair, literally lifting her off the ground, and tried to intervene, but she ended up being attacked as well, with clumps of hair being pulled from her head.

In early December we were taken back to court to hear what long-term fate Judge McCarthy had decided for us. We filed in, sat down on a bench and saw Mammy across the courtroom; she tried to smile at us but we could see the pain behind it and the sadness in her eyes. Trying desperately to look hopeful she mouthed a couple of words that we did not understand. Her look said *I love you* but the tears welled up in her eyes. We didn't spend long in there. Within minutes the judge had made up his mind. We were to be committed to somewhere called Mount Carmel Industrial School in Moate, County Westmeath, until our respective sixteenth birthdays. They were going to take away twenty-five collective years of our life.

Fifty years on I've seen the paperwork and the scant findings that allowed this theft that took away our childhoods and gave us criminal records instead. Mine just stated that I was illegitimate and that my previous character was 'good'. It gave my mother's weekly wage as twenty-three shillings and her weekly rent as six shillings. It also gave her widow's pension book number and the claim number of her children's allowance – which proved useful in making sure that she paid money over to the State for our keep. Her signature was never required for our committal.

The paperwork was duly filled in and the committal proceeding came to an abrupt end. Without another word being said, the three of us were ushered out by a court official. No one spoke. We didn't say goodbye to Mammy because we didn't know we were going direct from the court to the new school. I was stunned by what was going on. We were taken down some steps to the side of the courtroom and into a small waiting room. A door opened at once and suddenly we were outside, blinking and disorientated on an ordinary, dull winter's day.

Mammy, meanwhile, had been left on her own in the court-room. Realising that we weren't coming back, she jumped up and ran out after us, only to see us speed off in the back of the police car. I will never forget the sight of her, arms outstretched, rushing towards the car as though she was going to throw herself in front of it. But she didn't see the step and the next thing I knew she was falling forward, her hair all messed up and wild-looking, and she landed smack on her face. Our car was accelerating quite quickly now, but I could still hear her piercing scream. Sarah Louise put her hand over Lydia's eyes to shield them, but no one came to help Mammy and that was the last image I had of her as we were driven away.

Chapter 7

When I first went into Moate Industrial School, I was in a trance; I was walking as you do in your sleep. I remember the other children just standing, staring at us – the new girls. There were no smiles. No one was playing; no one was laughing. They were all dressed in the same drab clothes. There was just a sea of faces all looking blankly at me and my two sisters. A nun appeared to take charge of us and ushered us through the crowd. Annie Wogan just handed us over like parcels.

We went from the front hall along a very long passage into another room and one of the nuns told us to strip and hand over our clothes which were replaced with other ones. I started to feel very upset and said, 'Mammy gave me those clothes, they're my clothes,' and another nun told me harshly to shut up and took them away. I never saw my lovely Holy Communion coat with its velvet collar again. But they weren't satisfied with just taking our clothes away. They then cut all our hair off – Sarah Louise's long, dark silky hair, my blond ringlets and Lydia's mass of dark, wild curls – until we all practically looked the same with crude haircuts hacked off to above our neckline.

Sarah Louise dared to ask why we had to have our hair cut so short and one of the nuns curtly replied, 'Here, you don't ask questions. You are from the slums of Dublin, and you do as we say and as we want.'

We were given the regulation Mount Carmel uniform: a chemise made of the roughest, coarse fabric, a pair of hand-me-down, shapeless pants, a baggy skirt and an old jumper to wear on top. Someone glanced at our feet to make a rough guess at our shoe size and rummaged around in a huge box of old lace-up shoes to find something that would fit. Mine had big patches of mismatched leather on them where someone had clearly worn them right through. We were told that socks and knickers were washed every fortnight and then we were done, kitted out.

Having been shorn of our hair and our possessions we were now given a number. Mine was sixty. From now on I was not Kathleen O'Malley, a human being with her own personality, I was a number, which I was to use at all times because that was what identified me. I was to sew it in all of my clothes and inscribe it in any schoolbooks that I was given. After this we were sent upstairs and told to get ready for bed. It didn't matter that we had missed our tea. We would just have to wait until the next day to have something to eat. It didn't occur to anybody to ask if we were hungry or not and we did not dare ask.

We obediently followed the other girls upstairs to the second floor where a mass of girls were getting changed, still in total silence. We saw what the others were doing and took off our clothes, except for our chemise and knickers, and put them on the floor. Then we made a long queue into the washroom known (we were to learn later) as the big lavatory. This room had lots of little enamel basins set in a continuous metal stand which edged the whole of the room. We were told we each had our own basin which could be lifted off the stand and filled with water from the butler's sink where the tap was. We queued up and filled our basin with cold water then took it back to our stand and slotted it in. Initially I slopped it about as I tried to fit it in and a big splash of water tipped on to the floor but fortunately the nun in charge of us didn't seem to notice. Then I saw that the other girls were all cleaning their teeth first, not with toothpaste, just with their brush and water, so I set about doing that as best I could.

It was explained that after washing our teeth, we washed ourselves in cold water with carbolic soap. We did our hands, our arms, our underarms, our face, our neck, our ears. For modesty's sake we just did the upper section of our bodies. We kept our chemise on throughout the washing and just cleaned the bits you could see, making sure not to leave a tide-line because you would be in trouble for that. After this fairly strict routine of washing we dried ourselves on one of the coarse hard towels on the rail and then formed a line to present ourselves to the nun supervising – this was a Sister Ignatius – for inspection. She had been standing in the middle of the room throughout our wash making sure no one was fooling about or being immodest. When it was my turn, she explained that I had to show my hands palms downwards for inspection. She would then look at them, turn them over, then lift them up in the air so you were doing a kind of salute. I never did understand the last bit but Sarah Louise, who was more grown up than me, later told me that it was to check for signs of body hair, of puberty. She would then check behind our ears by bending them back, and the back of our neck in the thin silver below the hairline and above the chemise. She found a watermark on the girl who was in front of me and gave her a sharp slap across the face. 'Get back and wash yourself again,' she said. That first night, my sisters and I passed.

After this we combed our hair. I had noticed as soon as we arrived that all the girls were scratching their heads more or less constantly and I knew what that meant. Head lice were everywhere at Moate just as they had been at Goldenbridge and every day you were expected to comb your hair with the same fine-tooth comb that all the other girls had used. Sister Ignatius did random checks on this as well and anyone found with lice was punished. We didn't have lice when we arrived, because Mammy had eliminated them, but we duly pulled the comb through our hair then passed it on to one of the other girls.

Now it was time for bed. Sarah Louise and Lydia were taken off to St Brigit's, the top dormitory, while I was sent on my own to Our Lady's Dorm on the first floor. Iron beds were lined up top to tail just as they had been at Goldenbridge. I was handed a very large coarse nightdress and copied the other girls as they began to get undressed. This was not easy. I had to stand by the side of the bed, pull my nightdress over my head, let it drop and then take my jumper, skirt and my chemise off by pushing it up through the hole in the neck. I made a mess of it at first and saw one of the other girls scowling at me as I reappeared. Some part of me had clearly been on display and I could tell by her look that it was very important that nobody saw even a glimpse of your flesh whilst you were doing this.

After that we said our prayers with a strange, limping woman with a built-up shoe who told us she was a lay teacher and that her name was Miss Carberry. She slept in Our Lady's Dormitory with us to check that nothing bad was going on. Unsmiling, she ruled that room with a no-nonsense air. She had a little cubicle within the dormitory which had been sectioned off. It had walls which went about three-quarters of the way up, its own door and gave her a little privacy, though as she said to us, 'You might not be able to see me but I can hear everything that goes on.'

From early on I developed a real love-hate relationship with Miss Carberry. At times kind and apparently on our side, she was also the person who administered the night-time beatings when you wet the bed. And once I had spent a few lonely, cold nights in that room I – who had been dry at night for years – started wetting the bed with a vengeance. Very few nights passed without her beating me for it. She was not as fierce as many of the nuns at Moate but given that she was in charge of the dormitory and that was where the majority of 'crimes' were committed, she certainly gave out more than her share of punishments.

We were in bed by seven-thirty and at eight o'clock the last call went out: 'Anyone for the lavatory, line up now.' It was just up the stairs between both dormitories and a long queue formed to use it. Miss Carberry stood at the door watching and you simply went in, did your business and then out again without even flushing. Thankfully I noticed that toilet paper was provided and although it was the horrible crispy kind that didn't absorb much, at least it was better than having to use the walls as we had at Goldenbridge.

I lay on the thin hard mattress under the scratchy sheet and tried to will sleep to come. I had crossed my arms over my chest as Miss Carberry had instructed me to. 'That way if you die in the night, you'll be ready to meet God.' It was hardly a comforting thought but I did as I was told. I heard the other girls whisper to each other, 'Night, night, don't let the fleas bite.' I tried so hard not to feel miserable but as soon as the lights went out I started to cry. I cried because there was no one to talk to. I had been separated from my sisters and they were far way in the other dorm. I thought about the dawn raid at our house and poor Mammy having to let those horrible people in wearing only her nightdress. I cried because of going to the court and being taken away in the car. I cried because I was on my own and miserable and I knew we were as far away from Lower Bridge Street as I had ever been before in my life. But the room was freezing and I just couldn't sleep with my hands crossed on my chest, so I tucked the huge nightdress I had been given under my feet, then I lay on my side breathing hot air down through the neck hole, desperately trying to warm up my shivering body.

I felt so lost and alone even with the other girls around me. I hated the constant silence. The only time my voice had been heard that day was in prayer to Jesus and Mary but for once that hadn't comforted me either. My last thought before sleep finally came was that it was because of me that we'd all been locked up again; I was a very bad girl.

The following morning, a bell rang at 6.30 a.m. I was so disorientated I didn't even know where I was. Then it hit me and my stomach knotted up and I felt like crying all over again. Although it was pitch black outside and freezing in the dormitory we all clambered out of bed and fell to our knees to say our morning prayers out loud, led again by Miss Carberry. Then we got dressed. I took my nightdress off and was screamed at to put it back on. I was told to get dressed keeping my nightdress on so that I was completely covered. 'Chastity was next to godliness!' There was no question of washing. We simply pulled on our clothes from the day before and scuttled out to the nuns' chapel which was the other side of a small pebbled courtyard. A man called Father McKeon took the Mass. We knelt on a wooden step which was painful on my knees. I remember being told to keep still. But it was so uncomfortable. I knelt along with the other girls and tried to join in with the prayers in Latin even though I didn't understand them. I was so cold and still only half awake but I felt a glimmer of hope when I saw my sisters' heads in front of me and felt the vague comfort of something familiar.

After Mass we went back to the Industrial School for our breakfast. We queued up in silence and filed in to sit in silence at long tables presided over by Sister Ignatius. We had porridge, which was gritty and full of lumps and made with lots of salt, and a mug of very watered-down cocoa. I would have devoured anything, because I was so hungry, having not eaten the day before. But as it turned out I would not have had a choice as it was all we were ever given for breakfast, along with a slice of soda bread, and I learnt better than to leave even a scrape of it because if you did you would be beaten.

We called our lunch slop as it was just bits of disgusting jelly-like white fat floating about in watery gravy, with the odd vegetable thrown in – accompanied by the odd snail as the vegetables were never washed properly. Nothing was fresh and there was no variety.

Every day we went into the yard. We didn't go into the beautiful gardens that I had seen from the dormitory window and as we went to and from the nuns' chapel. Those immaculate lawns and carefully clipped flower beds were solely for the use of the nuns and the boarders who were in the other part of Mount Carmel convent and school. Our area, the space that we orphans (as we were called) were allocated, was not something you saw when you visited the convent. The yard where we took our exercise was a bare concrete square and there was nothing in it except a see-saw – no trees to climb or hopscotch marked out. There was a tap in the yard and we would duck under it to take mouthfuls of water. I tried to say something friendly to one of the girls and she just looked right through me. 'Will youse be quiet, in the name of God.' They leant against the nuns' railing and stared at me, saying nothing and doing nothing. Sometimes one of them would squat down on their hunkers instead; sometimes one or two words could be heard though it was hardly what you would call a conversation – they were usually insulting. One of the girls would pull another one's hair . . . that was usually the extent of our playground interaction.

Many of the children at Moate had been there since they were babies and had never known life outside the institution. In one way my sisters and I were lucky. At least we had had some time with Mammy. At first we tried to stick together when we could but gradually we began to stand by ourselves, hardly paying any attention to each other like all the other girls.

Yet the nuns always spoke of us as a group. One of them would sigh and say, 'The O'Malleys!' with a note of scorn or long-suffering. And they seemed to be saying, We know all about you so don't think you will get away with anything! They were always reminding us that we were the ones they picked up from the streets of Dublin and that we would be in the gutters if it weren't for them. Our fellow inmates were sharp. They did not know what we had done to end up there but they could see that the nuns thought little of the O'Malleys and that was enough for them to pick on us.

The nuns used any excuse to beat us: it could be for a mistake, if we dropped something, for example, or were bold or insolent – either asking a question or answering back or *not* answering. We were beaten for fidgeting, dragging our feet, and we were beaten for forgetting things. At first I was very shocked when I saw it happening, particularly if the transgression in question had just been an accident or someone being clumsy; such things had been rare at George's Hill. But quickly I saw what the others did and learnt to be cunning in order to avoid punishment. Girls would put the blame on others – would do anything if it would prevent them being the one beaten. We learnt to tell tales on our fellows as soon as we arrived. There was no comradeship, no solidarity, between us. Even the girls who had obviously been at the school for ages weren't friends.

The beatings were normally done in public. The nuns didn't call you away to punish you, they did it there and then, at the scene of the crime, in front of the other girls. They had a variety of weapons. For minor offences – sulking or having a bad attitude – they used their hands; for middling crimes – talking, having a water mark on your neck, a sock falling down – it was the ruler, which was permanently in the pocket of their habits. For the most serious offences – answering back or being defiant – the pointer, which was like a walking stick with a sharp end, was used. When they were being kind you were hit on the palm of your hand; when they wanted to chastise you harshly it was the back of your hands or the back of your legs. We had our ears boxed, our hair pulled, our faces slapped. If it wasn't you, it was the girl next to you. And as soon as we had a chance we did this to each other too. We learnt by example how to be cruel.

A lot of the punishments were given out in the refectory, during mealtimes, when the rest of the girls could see you and witness your shame. If you talked, or disobeyed a rule, or didn't eat the horrible food that was put in front of you, you were made to stand up so that everyone could see who the trouble-maker was. If you continued to be disobedient, you were called to the middle of the refectory and Sister Kevin would beat you, after which you were made to eat the food you couldn't stomach. If you still didn't do as you were told then you would have to climb up on to the window sill and stand up there. It was very high; you had to climb on the bench nearest the window, then hoist yourself up on to the sill. You had to stand there, not moving, for maybe half an hour. Sister Kevin would rub it in even further by saying, 'Look at her up there, she'd look nice on the Christmas tree, wouldn't she!' Then the other girls would laugh and make fun of you. And from that height you would be able to see and hear the boarders going past, happy and carefree. When you were allowed down you had to clear up after everyone and prepare the room for the next meal.

Once, later on, when I had misbehaved and caning was not deemed punishment enough I was sent off to St Joseph's Hall, which was a large area where the nuns had their lockers and which they had to go through to get from their cells to the refectory to the chapel. I was told to stand still with my hands by my sides and my back to the window, keenly aware that all the girls in the yard could see me and know that I was in disgrace. I stood there, burning up with shame, wishing I could make myself invisible. Every nun who passed by on their way to the nuns' chapel seemed to look at me with such utter disgust as though they weren't surprised that it was *me* giving trouble again. And it wasn't just the nuns who usually taught us at the Industrial School that I saw there that day. There were lay nuns who did the manual work around the convent, nuns I only ever saw at Mass, and nuns who taught the boarders, and they all filed past me and had a look. One tiny nun whom I'd never, ever seen before just shook her head when she saw me. 'Them O'Malleys. Sure they can't help it. They're rotten to the core.'

Moate was under the charge of Sister Ignatius when we first arrived. She was strict, but soon after Sister Kevin took over – and she was worse. She immediately threw all her energy into making our lives even more miserable, along with the help of Sister Bernadette. Sister Kevin supervised Moate with a rod of iron. She was about five foot eight or nine, and had a very imposing presence, despite the fact that she was only a novice at this point. She was unpredictable: it became clear from her first few weeks that she could be spiteful and cruel, but if you toed the line with her you were fine. Sarah Louise made the mistake of falling foul of her very soon after she arrived, and Sister Kevin hated her with a passion from then on. I quickly became very subdued, but my sister remained as feisty as ever and was on the receiving end of a beating most days. I worried because I knew it just gave the nuns further reason to hate the lot of us. Whenever she did something wrong, it reflected badly on me and Lydia. I started to resent Sarah Louise for drawing attention to us when all I wanted to do was to be invisible.

There were girls of all ages at Moate: from babies to fifteen-year-olds. As soon as I saw the area in the cloisters where the babies were, it reminded me of the Regina Coeli where Mammy had worked. It had that nice baby smell which I liked and it had a happier, noisier atmosphere than anywhere else at the school. I loved the contact with the little ones – just holding their hands or sitting with them on my lap – and quickly asked to help out whenever I could. Soon I was put in charge of feeding the babies. They had creamed potatoes every day which I had to feed them on a spoon. This was made properly like Mammy used to, mashed thoroughly so there were no lumps, then lots of creamy milk added. It tasted quite delicious. I would taste a bit to check it wasn't too hot, then I'd give them a mouthful and then I would taste the next spoonful, lick it till it was smooth; a spoon for them, a spoon for me. I would have to check first that there weren't any nuns patrolling outside in the grounds and then I would feed myself. I liked looking after the babies because I got to eat. I did it to survive.

After a year or two of watery porridge and slops I had become desperate. I saw what the other girls did when no one was looking and soon became a scavenger like them. There were outhouses where the potatoes and vegetables and dried peas were stored. Although these buildings had locks on them, we soon learnt how to pick them. Once the coast was clear I would nip in there and eat whatever I could get my hands on. The raw potatoes tasted bland even to a starving child, but the raw carrots and swede were like honey in comparison.

Outside the nuns' kitchen were the pigswill bins, where the nuns' leftovers were thrown. If no one was looking I would pick through it as quickly as I could looking for the fruit skins in particular. With the banana skins, I would remove any last traces of the fruit I could find, until I got to the slippery bit of the outside skin. I ate all the white pith from the orange skins, but never the rind itself because someone had told me it could give you jaundice.

I never knew if Sarah Louise or Lydia did this as well, but

I never thought of them whilst I was doing it or of trying to save some scrap to give them. My concern was for myself. That none of us girls cared about each other was one of the saddest things about Moate: I didn't care what was happening to my own flesh and blood so why would I care about girls to whom I was no relation? I longed for Chrissie Dumphy, my special friend with whom I had giggled and shared everything. In Moate nobody consoled you or hugged you or cheered you up when you were sad. You cried alone as you did everything else. I still cried in bed every night; it was the one place you could be alone with your feelings and let them out at all. Sarah Louise did try to help me once when she found out that I was wetting the bed. She sneaked into my dormitory one morning and showed me how to make the bed so that the wet patch was hidden and I would not be found out. But one of the nuns saw her on her way back to her dorm and she was beaten.

The only solidarity that anyone ever showed was when you went up to be beaten, someone might say, 'Don't let her make you cry. Don't let her think she's hurting you.' But you had to be careful even with this, because if the nuns saw you say something out of the corner of your mouth, you would be punished too. We'd deny that we had said anything, 'As God is my witness, I wasn't saying anything, sister, honest to God, sister.'

'Don't be blasphemous!' would be fired back and you got a clout anyway. You might as well have saved your breath.

Yet some did appear to get better treatment than others. There were a handful of girls known as the 'pets' who were treated with much greater leniency than the rest of us. Certain girls were never punished in all the time I was there. If two girls got into a fight and one of Sister Kevin's favoured ones was involved she would curl her bottom lip in a sneer and defend her pet. And that was not the only injustice: bullying was rife and the nuns seemed almost to take pleasure in the instances of viciousness displayed by their charges. A couple of years later, I was in a fight and had kicked the other girl quite hard. Sister Kevin heard about it and I expected all manner of punishment in retaliation. Instead she just said to me with a smirk, 'I believe you kicked Mary?' That was all; there was no beating. Perhaps it was the first time she had seen me show any spirit.

As well as physically hurting each other, we would hurl insults around and try to cause pain that way too. 'You're from the circus'; 'You're a tinker, a gom' – our vocabulary wasn't particularly large. My sisters and I were called 'dirty Dubliners' or 'Dublin Jackeens' because we had come from that city. Another word which was thrown around a lot by nuns and girls alike was '*amadán*', which was Gaelic for idiot. Not only did it mean you were a fool, it meant you were born to be a fool. If we got something wrong, the nuns would call us that and we would hurl it around between ourselves because we'd heard them using it so much. We were all *amadáns*.

When I first got to Moate I used to dream about running away as we had from Goldenbridge, but I never got very far because I didn't know where we could go. We had arrived by car after what seemed like a very long journey. The grounds were vast, and the fields beyond – the 'far fields' – extended as far as you could see. The big iron gate which did form an exit to the outside world was kept permanently padlocked. There was nowhere to go and after a while the thought no longer entered my head. The gate to the side of the convent was a metal gate painted black, it had a very small door set in it for deliveries or for the boarders to go down to the town and we used it to go out to Mass and for our walks. Some months into my first year, when the nuns were on retreat and Miss Carberry was looking after us, I remember finding that little door unlocked and so I opened it a fraction and peered out into the world. But all I could think of was: if I did step over – where would

I go? There was no point. Even if I did get out there were no draymen on the Guinness carts to give me a lift. I had looked for possible escape routes on our Sunday walks. Every Sunday after lunch we went out. We always walked along in threes with two of the nuns following us. Sometimes Sister Aquin came out with us and we always liked those walks the best because she was kind and pointed birds' nests and wildflowers out to us. We always took the same route: through the town passing a couple of closed shops, the butcher's, the parish church and a haberdashery. It was always quiet and still and we were told to walk in total silence when we went through the town. When we got to the country roads we could talk but when we were in public we had to appear very quiet and respectful. Sometimes we would pick blackberries. If you were at the front of the line, you could nip into the hedge, pull off a blackberry and then get back into line. Of course if you were caught you could look forward to a beating when you returned. But it was too difficult to resist the thought of eating fresh tasty fruit. Half an hour behind us the boarders would have their walk. They wore their uniforms with their navy blue mackintoshes and were a world apart from us in our shabby jumpers and skirts and old coats; there was no confusing the two. There was also a Technical School within our grounds: their girls went out last of all. It was carefully controlled so we never mixed.

I would see my sisters on those outings but we weren't allowed to walk together. Sarah Louise would be striding along confidently but Lydia always looked lost and frightened. Whenever I saw her around the school, she would be rocking back and forth continuously. Somehow I associated this strange rocking motion with what had happened when McCabe molested me and so I thought it was something bad, something to be ashamed of. Sister Kevin would speak to her very harshly and say, 'Lydia Byrne, stop doing that immediately!' and I knew the nun must be right and I prayed that my sister would stop doing it, stop bringing further disgrace on our family. I wanted to be sorry for Lydia but I couldn't.

Although I rarely had contact with Sarah Louise, she had power over me because I was sure she knew what I had done and whilst she may never have revealed it, I thought she *could* tell on me if she wanted to. Clearly Mother Malachy who was in charge of our admission to the school would have known about the attack and how I had been infected, but I worried constantly about who else knew. The nuns whom we had most contact with – Sister Kevin, Sister Bernadette, Sister Vincent, Sister Aquin – did they know? Only in adulthood can I reflect on how unlikely it would have been for them all to have known. A sexual attack would have been a taboo subject and not something they would have talked about. But that wouldn't have stopped them being curious, especially when I had to go back to court in Dublin. Sister Bernadette used to ask Sarah Louise about what happened, but she would just say, 'I've no idea, Sister. I don't know what went on with Kathleen. Mammy never told me.' And perhaps she really didn't know what had happened. She was only ten years old at the time and probably didn't question Mammy's lie about my tummy bug. Still, at the time the fear of who knew and what they might do with that knowledge haunted me and made my life more of a misery than it already was. I withdrew yet further into myself so as not to attract attention. I was totally lifeless – like a walking ghost.

Chapter 8

My return to Dublin happened quite soon after we arrived. Mother Malachy came to tell me that I would be going to court. I would be taken by car and must not tell anyone what it was about. I must not speak about Mr McCabe or repeat what I *claimed* he had done to me. And I would see my mother but I was not to speak to her until afterwards. She did not tell me what form the trial would take or if I would have to speak, only that I must not repeat the dirty things that I had said he had done. She said that if I was ever to receive God's forgiveness for my sins I would need to pray much harder than most of the girls because I had so much to repent. In a few short words she had convinced me of what I had been dreading: the nuns knew what I had done and they thought that I had caused it.

For the rest of that day I was treated with kid gloves. I knew I was being treated more kindly than usual and part of me enjoyed it, though I wished it could have been for another reason. When I went into the yard later I told my sisters I was going back to Dublin in the morning and would see Mammy.

It was to do with the problems over the tummy bug. Sarah Louise looked a bit put out that it was I going rather than her but said to send a message from her and Lydia that they were asking for her. I could hardly sleep that night. I felt sick and nervous but also excited. I was terrified of having to see Luke McCabe again but I desperately wanted to see my mammy.

Very early the next morning, well before dawn, Miss Carberry woke me up. She told me to get ready quickly and handed me a dress which was much nicer than my usual one. It had obviously been recently washed and pressed and I was just so surprised to have something clean to wear, I didn't ask any questions. I put the new clothes on, said my prayers and swallowed the piece of bread I was handed, though I didn't much feel like eating.

Sister Kevin was going to escort me in the car and the thought of that in itself made me feel really worried. I slept most of the way on the three-hour journey, but I do remember at one point Sister Kevin looking at me fiercely and drumming into me that on no account must I tell anyone about the bad things I had done. Clearly the nun I most feared knew what had happened and always had done. I started to feel really frightened. I thought Luke McCabe had done the bad things but now she seemed to be saying that it was *I* who was guilty, so what was I going to say in court if I was questioned? I felt very confused.

The trial took place at the Dublin Circuit Criminal Court on 9 February 1951. The building itself seemed huge and daunting; I remember little except looking everywhere for Mammy but not seeing her, then being told to go and stand up in the witness box and hearing the judge whose name was Joseph McCarthy reading out the charges against Luke McCabe. The first charge was that on 10 July the previous year he had unlawful carnal knowledge with me, Kathleen O'Malley, a girl of eight years; the second charge was that on that date, he attempted to have unlawful carnal knowledge with me; the third charge was that on that date he indecently assaulted me; and the fourth charge was that on that date he assaulted me, thereby causing me actual bodily harm.

The judge couldn't even swear me in because I was so young and nervous and when he asked me what would happen to me if I told a lie I answered that the Lord would light me. The judge then said, 'I won't swear this child, I have to be satisfied she appreciates the duty of telling the truth. I think she does, but I won't swear her.' It was a shaky start but he was obviously satisfied enough and let the counsel for the prosecution take over. After establishing my name, age and where I lived, Mr Mayne, the prosecutor, asked me once again to point to the accused in court, something I had hated when I had to do it before. This time around, without my mother there to protect and support me, it had even greater effect. I felt very agitated, so much so that by the time the questions became more specific about what actually happened that day, a lot of the time I was simply unable to answer the question at all.

Going through the transcripts as a middle-aged woman, I am transported back to what I felt like, a traumatised little girl standing up in court and clearly weighing up what I could and couldn't say. A lot of the time I am completely mute and there is a blank in the transcript. Mr Mayne clearly has to struggle to get me to describe anything that went on. Having clarified that on the day in question I ran an errand for Mr McCabe and when I came into his house afterwards he shut the door on me, after that I obviously don't know how to go on. After a great deal of questioning I say that the bad thing that he did to me was that he 'opened his trousers' and 'put me on his lap'. I cannot be more specific about the bad thing that he did, not in front of a courtroom full of complete strangers. After a great deal more questioning I say that he put one of my legs one side of him and one of my legs the other. I can't find words to describe the movement that he made, the horrible rocking movement. And the more the questioning goes on, the more incapable I am of saying what he did to me. I do not know the name for it – I am eight years old.

The questioning continues with no thought for what I might be going through at all. Eventually I say that he has his hands around me throughout and he was hurting me. Even this I find difficult to be specific about but in the end I say that the place that he was hurting me was below my waist. I just would not say what he was hurting me *with* although the questions from Mr Mayne went on and on. Sister Kevin's dire warning was ringing in my ears and I was determined not to bring any more shame on those around me.

What the all-male jury did not hear, but the judge and the prosecuting counsel had read before the trial, was my original statement that had been produced for the 8 August hearing. In that, I was much more explicit. I described how, after McCabe had opened his trousers, 'He took out his thing which he goes to the lavatory with in his hand. He put it into my wee. He was hurting me. I started to cry. He put it into me where I go to the toilet.' But now more than six months later I have a great fear of repeating those rude words in front of the judge so I don't say it.

Finally Mr Mayne's questioning ended and then I had to face cross-examination by McCabe's barrister, Mr Trant McCarthy. The tone was very different and the attempt to discredit my story was evident. After asking me what time I normally went to bed, where I lived and whether I played with Chrissie Dumphy, he then asked lots of questions about whether I hung around the local pubs and asked people for pennies. He then changed tack and asked why I didn't cry out more when McCabe allegedly attacked me. His final question was a strange one. He said it had all happened a long time ago and could I remember whether it was winter or summertime and I said it was winter (which of course was wrong).

The next witness was called. It was my mother. I don't think I had seen her before though I had scanned the court for her face when I arrived. I can't believe she sat through my own testimony. Yet, before being sworn in, my mother made the following statement, one that she must have thought about and prepared in advance. 'The little girl has been away in a school and the nun told her not to tell anybody about the dirty thing that was done to her.' I've seen that strange statement in black and white, but I have to wonder how she knew, let alone why she called me 'the little girl'. Was it to make it less real? Detach herself from the thought that it was her daughter who had been so badly abused? Had I managed to speak with her before we went in? Had she just guessed what had been going on behind the scenes? I can only think that like me she was being oddly formal because she was in court and like me, very nervous about having to stand up and make a statement under oath.

After that my mother's testimony was very straightforward. Mr Mayne simply wanted to ascertain what she had been doing on 10 July when the attack allegedly took place and what she had done on the days following leading up to the point when she noticed that I was unwell. There were no awkward questions and she must have done quite a good job because at the end the defence barrister chose not to cross-examine her.

Mrs Harris followed Mammy into the witness box and gave an even shorter account, confirming my sickly appearance by the fourteenth and confirming that she had washed my knickers the following day at my mother's request.

Then the doctors involved in the case were questioned. Their testimonies were crucial to its outcome. First on the witness stand was Dr Patrick O'Sullivan, who had first examined me on 14 July at St Stephen's Hospital. He gave an in-depth account of all the marks and abrasions found on my body: those on my chest, those running up to my armpit and those on my upper and inner thighs, about two inches down from my outer

genitalia. He described how my genitals were very inflamed
and as a result he was not able to examine them fully. He added
that he had examined the pus-like discharge coming from my
urethra and vagina which, examined microscopically later that
evening, 'revealed the presence of the organism of gonorrhoea'.
When the judge asked him how long he thought the infection
had been present, he said 'approximately three days'. Things
were obviously not going very well for the defence at this point
for Mr Trant McCarthy then asked quite a few questions which
hinted at the fact that in a laboratory as busy as the one Dr
O'Sullivan used, it would be possible for smears to get swapped
inadvertently or otherwise.

Dr Francis Bourke, the police doctor, was the next witness.
He said that as far as he could tell my hymen had not been
penetrated. Asked whether he noticed any bruises on me, he
replied, 'The child was crying. I don't think I examined her
otherwise.' When asked about the examination he had carried
out on McCabe, he stated that he had found a pus-like discharge
which on further questioning he admitted was suggestive of
gonorrhoea. He had taken two specimens of this emission and
given them in person to Garda Friel who was waiting outside.
When Garda Friel gave evidence, he confirmed that he had
indeed been given two separate sealed envelopes. These
contained specimen smears which he kept in his locker at the
police station until 17 July, two days later, before handing them
to Dr John McGrath, the pathologist.

McGrath's evidence was to be pivotal. Of the two smears
which had sat around in the policeman's locker for a couple of
days, mine did not show any evidence of the micro-organisms
present in gonorrhoea, only McCabe's sample did. Nor did the
(washed) knickers show anything. It would, of course, have
been a miracle if they had. Suddenly there was nothing to link
us. If I could not be linked forensically to McCabe then the
case would be thrown out because it would otherwise rely only

on circumstantial evidence and the testimony of a child. And that, as the judge later explained in his summing-up to the jury, was not sufficient in a court of law to condemn a man for such serious offences.

I just sat there listening. Finally Luke McCabe took the stand. His testimony was nonsense from beginning to end. He was confused about the date in July in question. He contradicts himself as to whether or not his wife was present and what exactly the message I was sent for was. A lot of his evidence rested on the presence of a third person in the room, a sick sister-in-law, who had since – conveniently – found herself detained in a sanatorium. He said that this invalid relative was the one who called out for Francie Byrne. And so it went on: a baffling account of who was called for and who was present. His wife Georgina gave evidence next. She was inconsistent about the time she reached home from her work at the Meath hospital. After her there were no more witnesses.

The judge in his summing-up stated that he had to point out that there was no evidence at all of rape. There was no evidence that there was any penetration of this girl's genitals, and the jury's first duty was to find the accused not guilty on count number 1, that the accused man had unlawful carnal knowledge of Kathleen O'Malley.

'That leaves the other charges open,' the judge then went on. 'Charges of this kind are very serious and if this man interfered with this girl and gave her gonorrhoea, it is a very serious thing.' He goes on to say: 'The important thing in this case on which the prosecution relies is that this child had gonorrhoea on the fourteenth of July and the accused man had gonorrhoea on the fifteenth of July and that the medical evidence says that she must have had it for two or three days. That is the important part of the case.'

The judge finally came to the end of his summing-up and the jury went away to consider their verdict. I stayed sitting, motionless, unable to make sense of what had gone on; to this day it remains mostly a haze. But I do remember sinking into myself, feeling everyone's eyes on me and knowing the trouble I had caused. I wanted to be swallowed up into the ground. When the jury reappeared I don't remember being aware of the fact that there were no women among them, no one who looked like Mammy or Mrs Harris – no one who would believe me.

The foreman read out their decision. Not guilty on the first count. Guilty on counts two, three and four. I didn't understand straightaway but then somehow it sank into my head that McCabe had been found guilty: I had been believed! He had been shown to be a liar and not me! Whilst he awaited sentencing he was sent to Mountjoy prison on remand. He would later be given twenty months in jail with hard labour.

I had no opportunity to see Mammy or speak to her. She tried to catch my eye when the verdict was reached. I could see her thinking, You see, we were right! We've won. But it was a hollow victory. I had been believed, but somehow I was still being punished and had to return to Moate to carry out the rest of my sentence.

Chapter 9

Something in me died. I just wanted to shut down and not feel anything. I didn't want to remember that man's face or where he had hurt me. My bed-wetting increased until it was almost every day that I would wake up to a urine-soaked bed followed by a beating from Miss Carberry, Sister Kevin or Sister Bernadette. In Moate it wasn't the girls who been there since they were babies who became the bed-wetters, it was the traumatised older girls like me who had arrived later. Every day it was the same miserable souls who were beaten for bed-wetting in the night; who then washed their sheets out in the laundry trying not to look at each other. Each day we hung them on the line to dry – only they didn't dry. I can still see my blue chilblained hands taking sheets off the line when it turned to dusk, to put them back, still damp, on to my still wet, permanently stained mattress.

In the morning, even if you'd wet the bed, you didn't wash; you just got up and got dressed; you didn't even clean your teeth as we always had done at home. You just got out of the bed and on to your knees and started to pray. Miss Carberry would direct us at these morning prayers, though we soon knew the words backwards. We would recite them out loud, making a big pretence of being far more awake than we really were. Every Sunday we got dressed and went to Mass in the nuns' chapel at 7am.

Then we had breakfast and did our manual work before going to the parish church at 11am to sing the Mass, leaving via the back gate. We walked in a long silent line. As it was early in the morning there would be hardly anybody around to see how dirty our clothes were because we wore our drab, worn winter coats tightly done up and no one came near enough to notice if we smelled bad.

We walked past the outhouses where the vegetables were kept and out through a little gate in the side. We were not to be confused with the boarders at the main school who left by the main gate.

I remember fainting a lot at Mass – whether through cold or hunger – and the only good thing about it was that you could stop kneeling and actually sit down. There was no medical treatment for it; sitting down was considered quite enough mollycoddling. Of course our meagre breakfast hadn't filled us up and we were still hungry. Often I felt I couldn't bear it. It was bitterly cold and the rumbling in my stomach as we knelt in the chapel would turn into a feeling of light-headedness and then I would keel over in a faint. The nuns never did anything about the problem of girls fainting despite the fact that it affected quite a number of us on a regular basis. To them it was probably just another sign of the uphill struggle facing them as they battled for our impure souls.

After Mass, then, and only then, were we given breakfast, though the fare was unvarying and nothing to look forward to. Then we all went off to our manual work, whatever we had been assigned to do: working in the refectory, the stairs, the workroom, the corridors, the cloisters, St Joseph's Hall, the kitchen, the sewing room, the dormitories, the lavatory, the nuns' chapel; all had to be scrubbed and polished on a daily basis. We were shown how to polish the floors the correct way with the cloths under our feet, using careful little movements. But when the nuns weren't watching, I followed the example of one of the older girls, and put the cloth under one foot only and zoomed up and down the hallway as though I was on a scooter. It was almost fun when you managed to get some speed up. Only after we had completed this first job would we be able to attend school. After school had finished we cleaned the primary school as well. As far as the nuns who oversaw us were concerned, this was all part of our training. It was essential to keep us occupied every minute of the day. And many of them clearly felt that educating us was a waste of time; cleaning was all we were fit for.

A short time into our stay I started itching constantly just as the other girls did. My head was alive with head lice and no amount of scratching would stop them. We tried to comb them out with a fine-tooth ebony comb which we dragged through our short, bristly hair. We did this every evening and I gradually started to get a bizarre thrill from catching them. It was disgusting, but satisfying; the *craic*, the feeling of pleasure when you got one – saw it on the comb – and killed it between your fingernails before it could escape. Then Sister Kevin did a random inspection and if she still found nits on your head, you'd get another beating, even though we were totally infested and never got rid of them entirely. I was one of the lucky ones, the white eggs were quite difficult to see on my blonde hair, but those with brown hair were targeted all the time by the nuns. But what could we do? We only washed our hair once a fortnight, we shared the same nit combs and the little things just climbed back and forth, back and forth between our filthy heads.

Bath night was once a fortnight on a Friday, at six in the

evening, once we'd finished our homework; everyone in the Industrial School bathed on the same day. There were five baths and seventy girls in total so that meant fourteen of us shared the same bathwater; we took it in turns to get in. You washed your hair first then had your bath, and the water became murkier and colder the closer you were to the back of the queue. You would undress leaving your chemise on for modesty's sake and put your clothes on a little bench. You never shut the door. At any time Sister Kevin could come in to look at you. Even though you were alone, you got into the bath with your chemise on, submerged yourself completely under water before pulling the now heavy, wet chemise over your head. A solution of Jeyes Fluid was put into the bath to disinfect us and turned the water cloudy. It was meant to get rid of the scabies and lice. There was a block of carbolic soap and we would wash our whole body in the bath, though we were discouraged from spending any time at all on our genitals. Then we would remove our filthy chemises and put a clean one on.

The summer of that year I started to feel the effects of a poor diet so acutely I literally dreamt of fresh, crisp, juicy fruit when I went to bed at night. Except for the scraps I managed to glean from the pigswill bin I never saw it and I simply longed for it. We saw apples daily – but we weren't allowed to touch them. They grew alongside the path we took every day to and from school. The old gardener whose name was Cavanagh watched over that area of the garden like a hawk. He knew what we were like – he'd had years of it. And although I knew the risks, something about those beautiful red apples used to cry out to me – *Come and get me! Come and eat me!* – and I would simply have to have one. Although there was always a nun at the front and the back of the line, if you were in the middle you had a chance. All the girls did it. If there was a windfall on the ground, I would do a quick check for Cavanagh and if the coast was clear, would jump into the bedding area, grab it and quick as lightning put it up the leg of my knickers. I would then continue on nonchalantly as though nothing had happened. Nine times out of ten, a crabby voice would shout – 'Put it back, yer tief!' – and that grizzled old face would appear from nowhere with a triumphant look on it. I would then be forced to stop, produce the apple and hand it over to him.

If you did manage to get an apple past Cavanagh, the only place you could eat it was in the dormitory at night. When all was silent, you bit into it quietly, muffling the crunching noise under the blanket. If Miss Carberry heard any rustlings she would immediately get up, leave the sanctity of her cubicle, her hair flying, hardly able to see without her glasses and tripping herself up without her special shoe. Looking like a wild witch she would stand between the beds demanding that the culprit make themselves known. As if you would own up! No one ever did – you weren't going to give up that delicious sweetness lightly. There would be total silence until she returned to her bed once again and then you would continue munching.

I was always hungry, always cold and always on the lookout for scraps. Every afternoon in the pantry, Sister Kevin would prepare the cocoa for supper; in an enamel bowl she mixed the cocoa powder, sugar and milk ready to add it to the huge urn of boiling water. There was enough to feed seventy girls once it had been highly diluted. Usually the pantry door was then locked but not on every occasion: sometimes Kevin would be distracted by a commotion elsewhere and rush out without properly securing it. Ever hopeful, I would check the door and if it was unlocked, pop my head round the corner, my body half in and half out of the pantry ready to make a quick getaway. I would pick up the wooden spoon that was permanently left in the big bowl and slurp up as much as I could of the cocoa mixture all the while keeping an eye and ear out for the swish, swish, swish, click, click, click of the rosary beads, which signalled the return of Sister Kevin or Mother Malachy. I'm sure I wasn't the only girl who did this, but it was one of the few crimes that actually seemed worth a flogging to me. Perhaps the nuns did realise that a thief was on the loose – the level of mixture in the mixing bowl had gone down dramatically – and perhaps that's why the pantry was sometimes left unlocked in order to catch them red-handed. But no one ever did get caught. The only ones to suffer were the other orphans, who had to put up with the cocoa being even more watered down than usual. But it was dog eat dog in there: as when I ate the babies' potato, I was just doing what I had to in order to survive. There were also large pottery jars full of jam and covered with muslin cloth. I would eat handfuls of it and feel sick, but again, it was worth it.

However much cocoa mixture I managed to drink, it was never enough. My overwhelming memory of Moate is of going to sleep hungry and cold, curled up in a tight little ball in a vain attempt to warm up. You were always cold and you soon realised that was a fact of life. No one was going to throw another blanket on you or a nice warm coat like Mammy used to. Wetting the bed warmed you up but not for long, the urine soon turned cold and then you'd be dragged out of bed for a beating. Whilst we did have a sort of basic central heating system with a furnace downstairs, housed in what was known as the crudery room, which we had to keep stoked up with turf, it just didn't kick out enough heat to get the rooms at all warm. The dormitories had very high ceilings, draughty windows with no curtains and the radiators were so spaced out they couldn't begin to cope. We were cold in bed and out of it; it seeped into your bones after a while.

The boarding school, where the daughters of nice middle-class families were sent, was right next door to us, but a world apart from where we orphans slept and went to school. The grounds were beautiful: landscaped flower beds surrounding an elegant emerald-green lawn. There were always nuns out there pruning the roses and tending the vegetable patch, weeding or maintaining the nuns' graves which were in a section of the garden which was apparently consecrated ground. But we were always kept well away from this part and it was made extremely clear that we must never, ever mix with the boarders whose place it was. We had nothing in common with them anyway, we were third-class citizens and no communication was allowed.

Needless to say the boarders' food was far, far better than ours; we knew it was because we sometimes got a glimpse of what they threw away. Everything about their day-to-day existence was a world apart. If the food had been at all similar then their nice middle-class parents would just have taken their children somewhere else. We kept an eye on their rubbish bins accordingly. If the boarders threw out food – a half-eaten apple core, a piece of biscuit which had gone soft – we would find it in their bins when we were going past and eat it ourselves. We had to be very careful because those bins were strictly out of bounds to us, but often you were so famished you didn't care about the repercussions.

There was also a National School – a day school – on the same grounds. If the day pupils didn't go home at lunchtime, they brought in their own sandwiches, which they ate in the domestic science rooms. One day one of the orphans was caught taking a crust which had been thrown away out of there. One of the elderly nuns caught her, accused her of thieving and shouted at her, 'That food is for the poor children. You're a robber.' The orphan was taken off and beaten; the leftover was taken off her. You never got a reprimand without a physical attack as well; they went hand in hand. The rumour about what had happened went round in its usual dull, bored way in the yard the next day, but I couldn't even pretend not to care. I kept thinking, Who was poorer or more deserving than us; why could they not see what was right under their noses?

The nuns used to tell us stories to set the fear of God in our hearts and keep us on the straight and narrow. When there was thunder and lightning the nuns told us that it was God's way of showing that he was angry with us. The only mirror in the school was in the cloisters and it was turned inwards as soon as an electric storm was predicted. Even when it was turned back round again we still weren't allowed to look at our reflection. The nuns would get their ruler out immediately and accuse you of vanity if you were caught, which we always thought was a bit strange because some of the nuns looked at themselves regularly as they passed by.

The nuns told us about the work of their missionary sisters in Africa converting the barbaric natives who were no better than monkeys. We were always being told to pray for the black babies who had the misfortune to be born wild savages and who were even further away from good then we were; there was even a little collection box left in our classroom with a faded picture of a black baby on it. As wretched as my existence was, here were children worse off than I was! What had they done to deserve such a poor life? I wondered if they were as bad as the Protestants.

Anyone living outside Holy Catholic Ireland, particularly those who had the misfortune to go to England, were mentioned in our prayers because they had gone to a pagan land where there were Protestants. We used to pray very hard that they didn't lose their souls. After all, what could be worse than a Protestant? We had been saved, we were chosen; we must remember those who were not as fortunate as we were.

One day the nuns told us a terrible story which had made the headline news of a child who had been kidnapped, stolen from her pram in broad daylight. It had quite a profound effect on me. I was only a little girl myself and we were on our knees saying the rosary, praying and feeling very sad for this bereft mother and hoping against hope that her baby would be found.

But it never occurred to me, or at least not until many years later, that we had effectively been kidnapped ourselves – taken from our mother against her will.

Generally I listened to the stories from the catechism and took them entirely at face value; we weren't encouraged to look for any deeper meaning or relevance. But the nativity was always very puzzling to me. I used to question to myself the scene in the stable with Mary and Joseph and the baby Jesus in the crib. I tried just to see the story as others seemed to, as the humble beginnings of our saviour Jesus Christ but I looked and looked at those pictures and couldn't dismiss the voice in my head which said, It wasn't even a proper room! Deep down I just couldn't understand how Jesus could have been born in such poverty. Surely a bed of straw alongside the animals really was being destitute, which is what they'd accused us of being. I couldn't understand why Mary was so revered if she was so poor and my mother wasn't respected at all. I found the whole story very troubling and contradictory. Christmas was always a difficult time at Moate. It was the time of year we had been taken away from home and it was filled with sadness and confusion, though it was the one day a year when the nuns made an effort, a small one, to treat us like normal children. We woke on Christmas morning to an orange and lollipop at the bottom of our beds, which had been placed inside our torn, smelly socks. But it was a whole orange and nothing has ever tasted as sweet before or since. Breakfast was a skinless sausage and a piece of black pudding and best of all it was the one day a year when the silence was broken. We could talk all day and we did! We couldn't believe our luck. We kept saying, 'Aren't the nuns good to us! Wouldn't it be nice if Christmas came every day!'

We had a couple of letters from Mammy during our first year but that was all. They were brief and sweet and said nothing about her or 29 Lower Bridge Street, only that she hoped we were doing well at our lessons and saying our prayers. They were signed with *lots of love, your mammy*. I knew that we were being kept well away from her because the NSPCC inspector had said we had to be. Because no one spoke about her, I resigned myself to my orphan state; sometimes it truly seemed as though she really hadn't existed at all. One day in my first year though (I never knew which month it was, only that it was warm and sunny outside), one of the nuns surprised me by saying, 'Your mammy is here to see you.' There was no warning, no looking forward to the visit; it was just as though she'd turned up there out of the blue. 'Go and get Lydia and Sarah Louise,' she said.

The three of us were herded up and told we must put on fresh dresses and have our hair combed; we needed to be tidied up a bit. It was the first time we had been lumped together and treated like sisters for months. We were taken down to the parlour in the convent which I had not seen since we arrived. It was very bare except for a little table and a chair and there was Mammy, sitting down, only she didn't see us when we walked in because she had Paul on her lap and was staring hard at the floor.

Sarah Louise and Lydia and I stopped just inside the door and stayed there looking at Mammy and she looked at us. She'd seen me from across the courtroom back in February but this was the first time she'd seen all of us without our lovely long hair. We'd almost got used to our shorn locks but it was obviously a great shock to her and her eyes filled up with tears. Now, we'd been told by the nuns that under no circumstances were we to upset Mammy, and she told me years later that that was exactly what they had also told her. So she sat stiffly at the table, in her smart suit that was so familiar, and, though I longed to reach out and touch her, I didn't do anything; we just stood by the door frozen like statues.

Mammy had been told not to worry or upset us, but she obviously hadn't counted on us looking as bad as we did. She had almost convinced herself that we were away at a boarding school being looked after by the lovely kind sisters, as she had told other people. She just hadn't expected us to look so institutionalised. The last time she'd been with us, Sarah Louise was a real tomboy, I was inseparable from my dolly and Lydia was just a little girl. Now we looked more or less the same – thin and pale and fearful, and it had only been a few months. Mammy was obviously trying to contain herself but she started to cry and to this day I remember a big drip collecting on the end of her nose. I felt quite concerned about that. I wanted to tell her but I didn't; I couldn't say anything. There was a nun just outside the parlour door which had to remain open and I was scared to speak. I remember that visit very clearly though I don't remember any dialogue really passing between us. I wanted to look at Mammy to try to memorise every detail of her appearance and save it for later. I remember thinking the nuns would be impressed by her neat outfit and they would see she was the best mammy in the whole of Ireland.

Still no one said anything. After a long pause, we started – almost as a pack – to sidle up to Mammy. I think she had put her hands out to us, and I remember leaning up against her and feeling her warmth and smelling her smell; it was a forgotten feeling of comfort and safety. And because she was crying, I started to cry, but I did it quietly, like she did, so the nun wouldn't think that I was upsetting her.

The visit didn't last very long. I doubt it was as long as an hour. Suddenly Sister Agnes was back in the room and making it clear that it was time for us to go back to school; the visit was over. It had been horribly painful; a very awkward silence with nothing to fill it. Mammy who had always touched us, hugged us, cuddled us, had sat for most of it very formally in a stiff little chair. She had looked concerned at our appearance and that had reminded me how bad we must look. When the nun came in she asked why our hair had been cut. 'Oh Mrs Byrne, the children's energy goes into their hair so we keep it short.' We were probably all a bit relieved. We did our best to show that, as instructed, no one had upset anyone, no one had made a scene and then Mammy gave us each a little bag of sweets and a present each, and we said our formal goodbyes. Once we were out of earshot of the parlour, Sister Agnes told us to go back to the orphanage where we changed back into our ragged old clothes.

Later in the yard all the girls came rushing up to us. They knew we'd had a visit and they crowded round us and asked could they mind our sweets for us? It gave me a feeling of satisfaction knowing I had something they wanted. 'Can I have a lick of your lollipop?' I never thought of the germs, just that they were being nice to me – even it only lasted as long as the sweets.

Chapter 10

Every year we were given new schoolbooks. These weren't really new, they were dog-eared and tatty; they had been passed down from year to year, from orphan to orphan. We were given nice shiny, crisp brown paper to cover these schoolbooks at the start of the academic year and the corners had to be exact and I had to keep on practising until I got it perfect. On the front we had to write our names in Gaelic. So I wrote out carefully *Caitlin Ni Maille*.

We were in the heart of the country and Gaelic was what we had to study most subjects in. There was a huge pride in all things Irish at the time, particularly among the Sisters of Mercy, and speaking and understanding our native language was drilled into us from a young age. Although we prayed in English and Latin and counted in English, most other subjects were conducted in Gaelic and that was the start of my downfall. We had never spoken it at home, and although my older sister took to it like a duck to water, I just couldn't seem to learn it. Although quite often I could understand what was being said in Gaelic, there was simply too much going on in my mind to remember it properly when it came to writing and composition.

When I went into the second class, we had Sister Gerard to teach us, who only needed the slightest provocation to give us a beating. She was infamous for her short temper. She wore her wedding ring, as all the nuns did, but unlike the others she used it as a weapon. If you breathed wrong she would hammer you on the skull with it. She waited for you to fidget or drop something and she was straight down the aisle ready to hammer you with the hard ring. It was her own special form of punishment – perfect for instilling law and order into dirty girls whom she was wasting her time trying to educate. That piece of jewellery which was meant to symbolise her marriage to God was used as a method of torture on children.

If you wrote with your left hand you were thought to have been touched by the devil and you were known as a *kitogue*, an imbecile. But you weren't allowed to remain a left-hander, you were forced to write with your right hand, however awkward it was. Being left-handed was seen as freakish and the devil's work and it had to be corrected. There was a dunce's corner in every classroom and it was frequently used, by me as much as anyone.

I wasn't sorry when it was announced that certain girls would be given jobs to do during what had traditionally been school periods: I saw it as a break from that hateful Gaelic which continued to defeat me. At eleven o'clock Sister Magdalene, or Sister Cecilia who took us for the singing of Mass, would call out for 'peelers' to prepare the potatoes. That meant you were dismissed from class and a little bit closer to the food, so there were usually quite a few volunteers. Potatoes were peeled, then scrubbed in the troughs in the back yard with a large scrubbing deck, before being put to soak in cold water. We always did enough for two days and enough potatoes for the whole school. Often by the second day the potatoes were going off a bit but they were still boiled up and served and we had to eat them. Being a 'peeler' was hard work; it was a huge job that seemed never ending but it was worth it to get out of Gaelic.

Nobody had any expectations that we orphans could learn anything anyway. We weren't encouraged to read. We were given books for the duration of the lesson only: they were to be handed back at the end. At one point I remember Sister Aquin trying to get reading books for us but it fell on deaf ears. Occasionally Sarah Louise would get a comic from her friend Mary and they would read these under the bedclothes, never in public. You had to sneak reading material in and pass things on, and I just couldn't work up the necessary enthusiasm. Mammy had sent me a catechism early on and that was my only book. I would read that and practise my ten commandments rather than risk being caught with banned books. Every day we learned the catechism in school and every night I would look at the catechism from Mammy and hope that a bit of it might rub off on me.

At the age of ten, my education, such as it was, dwindled down to three days a week because on Monday and Wednesday I would leave the classroom at ten o clock to go to the laundries. I did the roll call (to please the school inspectors), said my prayers, class commenced and then it would be 'Laundries?' 'Peelers?' and that was more than half us orphans done for the day.

We worked in the laundry from ten in the morning till two in the afternoon two days a week and it was hard, sweaty work. The laundries were contained in a large single-storey building which opened out on to the cement yard where we played. The door on the left contained the ironing room which was often locked. It had a shiny black range which we stoked with turf at one end of it where the irons were heated and six long tables where the sheets were ironed. We had to keep the range burning in order to provide constant heat for the irons lined along it. As the iron you were using cooled down, you would return it to the range and pick up a hot one.

Sister Bernard ran the laundry and you were not allowed to be there unless she was. The laundry contained the most enormous industrial washing machine and she guarded this with her life. It had a vast brass lid with a handle which only she could unlock from the key she always had attached to her belt. The furnace for the laundry was housed in what was known as the crudery room, out in the back yard. We had to keep it stoked with turf in order to have constant hot water. When we had baths, the procedure was the same.

There was also an area where the hand-washing was done: a long row of old butler's sinks, yellowish in colour, and chipped in places. They fitted a scrubbing board and that was where we girls would stand, washing the socks, knickers and chemises with a big bar of carbolic soap. Some of the girls would be washing their sheets in the footbath to get the stains out before hanging them out behind the outhouses where there were clothes lines. There was a big mangle in there which took four girls to manage and we used this to try to get some of the water out of the sheets and the large items before hanging them up. The boarders' and the nuns' sheets were hung up on huge drying racks above our heads that you raised and lowered.

We did the orphans' washing and the boarders' washing, but we weren't considered pure enough to touch the nuns' clothes: they were sacrosanct. One time I did see a pair of the most enormous black bloomers in the laundry, and I pointed them out to the girl washing next to me and we got the worst giggles. That was what they wore under those huge habits! They were vast things, several of us could have got into one leg of them and still had room left over. We never laughed together but that day we couldn't stop. We knew we would get a sound beating later but it was worth it. It was my one and only sighting of a pair of nun's knickers. I never did see a habit being washed and often wondered if they spent their entire lives in the same one without it going near a bar of soap.

Once we'd finished the washing we cleaned the laundry, polishing the big metal lid of the machine with Brasso, drying off the mangle and putting it away, scrubbing the boards and basins and polishing the red quarry tile floors till they shone. The range had to be blackened with polish then rubbed with a soft cloth till you could see your face in it. Everything was left immaculate. It was part of our training for the future. If anyone was ever overheard complaining about anything they would say they were keeping us occupied, that a spirit of industry was to be fostered in the young, it was one of the founding principles of the Industrial Schools.

I often did the washing at the sink next to a girl called Maureen Slevin. She was my year and very pretty. She was also much better at schoolwork than I was and would let me copy from her book; she was nice like that, a kind and thoughtful person who hadn't become hardened by the system.

Sometimes we were able to have a small chat when we were scrubbing the clothes and Sister Bernard was out of earshot. We would talk about our life before the school, about our families. Maureen was one of four children and her mother had died in childbirth when she was little and they were brought up by their grandmother until a priest advised their grandmother to let the 'good holy sisters' look after them.

The 'good holy sisters' rarely had a good word to say to us and only sometimes would they make a routine enquiry about your welfare. Our answer would always be simple and the same. 'I'm fine thank you, sister.' The one exception to this was a lay nun called Sister Monica who oversaw us and did the work with us in the ironing room.

The ironing work was very repetitive: you took a heated-up

iron from the stove with a cloth so as not to burn your hands then ironed the sheets on the huge work tables. When that iron had cooled down you put it back on the stove and took another one. At some point during this process I remember asking Sister Monica very innocently whether when she died she would come back and visit me. I was very fond of her. I wanted her to tell me where she had gone and what it was like. She may well have been quite surprised by this – she was only of middle years herself at the time – but she said lightly that she would try to. When I asked her to promise, she said she couldn't because she couldn't make a `promise that she might not be able to keep.

I think that was the deepest conversation I ever had with anyone there. I felt able to open up with her, for she was the only nun I could say I liked. She was different to the other nuns and never cruel.

By the time we'd finished in the laundry, we were usually red-faced and soaked with perspiration, but still we didn't stop. Once it was tidy, we went straight to wherever we were cleaning at that time. Sometimes it was the dormitory, sometimes it was the classrooms; we all had our tasks assigned to us and each year it changed. Every autumn the manual duties rota was posted up on the notice board. This was met with great excitement and we would crowd round the board, pushing each other out of the way, looking to see what we had been put down for.

When we weren't working in or around the school, we were out in what was known as the far fields. The convent was very wealthy and owned most of the land as far as the eye could see and it was our job to weed the rows of crops and pick them when they were ready. I remember as though it were yesterday the first time we went out there. I had just finished my cleaning job when I found Sister Kevin lining a group up in the yard. 'We're going out to the far fields,' she said. 'Take off your school clothes and fold them. You will wear these.'

She handed each of us a pile of filthy rags. 'Leave your shoes here; we don't want them getting muddy and spoilt.' The clothes stank of sweat and were stiff with mud and putting them on was one of the worst things I had ever had to do, but I was very fearful of Sister Kevin and did as I was instructed, lining up in my rags and bare feet. I was deeply embarrassed and prayed silently to God that we would be spared the humiliation of anyone seeing us. When everyone was ready Sister Kevin led us out in a long line behind the orphanage and past the boarders in their classroom all the way out to the far fields. It was a long way and our feet were soon scratched and cut from the stones and brambles on the path. When we got there we were shown row upon row of vegetables and potatoes and told that it was our job to harvest them. We were to pick them carefully and put as many as we could carry into our skirts before taking them down to the big pits which had already been prepared for us where they were to be buried. (Later I overheard someone say the holes were so deep to make sure the light wouldn't get to the vegetables and they would survive the winter intact.)

The older girls, who had done it before, went scuttling off up and down the rows, throwing vegetables into their skirts and carrying them this way and that. It looked like back-breaking work but at the same time it was just so nice to be outside the walls of the orphanage; I breathed in the luxury of the fresh country air and a nice memory started to come back to me of being out at Bohernabreena when I was just a little girl, but as if Sister Kevin had read my mind she barked out, above the wind rustling through the field, 'I will be watching you at all times. Is that clear?'

'Yes, sister,' we chorused back.

During the harvest we went out every day to the far fields. Sister Bernadette or Sister Kevin were always out there with us. We were never without supervision. The farmer who looked after the land was sometimes out there too but he might be called off to milk the cows or help with the sheep; the nuns were a constant: their beady eyes bore into you whatever you were doing. We lifted potatoes and swedes, cabbages and carrots, and all the time those eyes followed you to check you weren't dropping them or larking about. We picked and carried there every day till our arms were ready to drop off and there was no more light to see by. Once each crop was harvested we would move on to something else. It was often very cold by the end of the day but we were never allowed to put on our shoes.

Sometimes, while we were picking the vegetables, we would actually chat to each other, which was something we never did normally. I think there was something about being out in the fresh air with the wind blowing around us that freed us up to behave a bit more like normal children. And whenever you got the chance, if you were bent right down low over the crops and were sure you couldn't be seen, you'd have a few sneaky bites out of a carrot, swede or a potato – whatever was available. And Sister Kevin and Sister Bernadette seemed to treat us with a bit more leniency when we out there than they ever did around the school.

During harvest times we went out after school and didn't get back till after dark. If there was a field of potatoes to pick, we picked until it was done and we would be rewarded with a hot piece of fruit pie, apple or rhubarb, when we got back. The thought of that pie kept us all going and probably able to do all that hard labour. Sometimes it made our tummies hurt a bit because we weren't used to such rich food, but it was worth the pain.

Back at the school we were allowed a footbath when we came in because our feet were so cold and chilblained. The bath itself was in the laundry and was normally used for washing sheets. It was about three or four metres long and we all sat on the side and dipped our feet in the lukewarm water at the same time. The Jeyes Fluid stung a bit but still it was a pleasant feeling swishing your feet about and feeling the soreness ebb away.

Once we'd soaked our feet and washed our hands in carbolic soap, we had to step out of our farm clothes, fold them up stiff with dirt from the fields and put them away till the next day. We then got back into our school clothes. If Sister Kevin had found these had been left crumpled up when we went out to the fields, she would make a note of that girl's name on a list. Once I was in a hurry and left mine untidily and she said to me, 'You will get six slaps on your hand for that, but you can choose which hand you would like it on.' All the time during the tea when I was having my bit of soda bread and mug of cocoa and looking forward to a slice of tart, I couldn't stop thinking of the punishment I was going to get, and which hand I would like it on, as though that were a choice at all! I lined up to see Sister Kevin afterwards, getting more anxious by the minute. I held out my left hand and she hit me with a ruler several times hard on the back of my hand. It stung particularly badly because my hands were already red raw and chilblained from picking the vegetables.

Even when the crops were all harvested, we continued working out in the fields often as late as November, weeding the rows, sowing the seeds and clearing up the stones ready for ploughing. Our fingernails were black with the farm dirt and the quicks round the edges split and caught on everything, which was really painful. We went out to the fields from the start of the harvest when it was mild and often sunny and didn't finish till late in the autumn when there was frost on the ground.

Apart from keenly feeling the humiliation of walking by the boarding school dressed in rags, I was also jealous of what they were being taught to do, while we were considered suitable only for hard labour. Whenever I passed their tennis courts, I fantasised that one day someone would suggest that

I learn to play, that someone would think me worthy of learning a skill.

But my misery would lift a little when we got a ride on the farmer's trailer out to the fields. At least I was away from the school for a while and we would be out in the open air and we could pretend to be free. We were dropped at the edge of the fields and then we would have to walk to wherever we were picking that day; it could be for miles – in our bare feet, of course. It was a very large farm covering acres and acres of land. If we got there ahead of Sister Kevin, we'd run up and down the rows messing about and then the farmer would shout at us to stop playing and start picking.

Age never came into it: all little hands could pull weeds and pick potatoes. And weeding was an all-year-round activity: even when it was freezing we went out to tidy up the lanes in the fields. Then there were the deliveries of turf. A lorry would turn up and dump a whole load in the yard and we would have to throw the bricks of dirt into the shed. It was a huge job; it went on for days. Occasionally when no one was looking we managed to make a game of it – running up and down the mountain of turf and pretending we were somewhere else. There was dust everywhere and it got all over our clothes and skin, under our fingernails and in our hair; it was dusty and filthy and we scratched and scratched. Sometimes, when we came back from the far fields, we were literally covered from head to toe.

Whilst I was jealous of the boarders' privileges, I also envied the girls who attended the Technical School. Aged between sixteen and eighteen, they had been sent there to learn farming and domestic science. Unlike me, they were gaining proper skills and looked organised and tidy when I saw them performing their tasks. We were never allowed to mix during termtime, and when they went home for the holidays we took over their manual work. This meant feeding the turkeys and chickens, cleaning out their pens and tending the vegetable patch. We would also churn the milk in a huge vat to make the butter. I remember churning and churning it, then patting the butter with the wooden bats and shaping it into little rolls for the nuns. Whilst we were given only the merest scrape of butter on half a piece of soda bread each day after school, the nuns enjoyed it at all their meals and we produced a fair amount of butter for them. And whilst the Technical-School girls might have looked after the turkeys, feeding them and so on, all year, when it came to Christmas and the actual killing and plucking of them, that job was left to us orphans. It was a hateful task. It was done on the farm; it was always bitterly cold, our hands were frozen and clumsy and we had to break their necks by pulling them hard over a broom handle. The fowl would scream as you did it. Then the feathers needed really yanking to get them out. Even with Christmas looming, there was little for us orphans to get excited about, so we sat there taking our anger out on the turkeys and talked about nothing. Somehow being there doing the Technical girls' dirty work made everything even worse and highlighted the differences with the work we usually did. This farm where the Technical girls learnt their farming skills was totally different to the far fields where we picked potatoes and weeded; it had acres and acres of fertile land, lots of costly machinery and animals and was unbelievably wealthy.

So we resented the Technical-School girls. Whilst their living arrangements weren't quite as posh as the boarding-school girls', they lived in nice surroundings and their parents were allowed to visit on Sundays. And, unlike the manual work we did, the manual work that *they* did was going to get them a qualification. It just all seemed so unfair.

Once, I was stacking piles of clean linen away in the tank, which is what we called the cupboard it was stored in, when

I heard someone playing the violin in the infirmary. The music didn't sound lovely to me. In fact, it made me quite upset because I knew that Sister Cecilia was teaching one of the girls. Sister Cecilia was a talented musician; she could play the harp and the cello amongst other instruments. I stood on the steps leading up to the infirmary and burned with the injustice of it all. I wished so much that it could be me. I busied myself cleaning the steps and polishing the door, and yearned with every bone in my body to change places with her. As I listened to the same piece of music being played over and over again, I felt a huge wave of sadness that I was only chosen for drudgery. Why did nobody ever see any potential in me? Why was I always working in the fields or washing or scrubbing?

I wanted to be good at something. I wanted to be an artist at one stage and I was allowed to ask mammy to send me some paints. I used to get them out and paint whenever we were in the workroom making things for the sale of work. Sister Bernard told me there was to be a competition in the forthcoming sale so she drew the outline of a little ship on a postcard-sized piece of paper and I coloured it. It got first prize and I was delighted. I wasn't allowed to claim my prize. The nuns took the money and kept it. To make matters worse the painting was sold and I never saw it again.

When I'd first arrived we'd just taken an old, coarse jumper out of a great big bin, worn it every day until the following summer, when it was finally replaced with a summer dress. This happened for a year or two. Then I was told that as a reward for being a good girl and behaving myself, I would be allowed to knit my own jumper. I was delighted. I had already knitted socks – we did that on four needles in the round with thick grey wool, and I felt I was rather good at it. Our jumpers were generally grey and red (though that depended on what the nuns could get hold of cheaply) and had a round crew neck, so it was quite a skilled job; you really had to concentrate. You had to do two rows, knit and purl, in one colour, then you used the other colour for the next two rows. When you'd finished that you did the grey bit round the neck. It took me a long time to knit that jumper and I was pleased as Punch the first time I put it on. It was so much softer than the ones I had previously been given, which had been handed down repeatedly and probably boil-washed to get rid of the germs. I still had to have a second-hand chemise from the clothing bin but suddenly it didn't feel quite as bad now the top half had been improved. I felt quite proud of my effort. Then I sewed my number sixty into it. When I wore it I couldn't help looking at myself in the mirror whenever I got the opportunity to go down to the cloisters.

We had two pairs of socks and we changed them once a fortnight. They used to be rock hard and so smelly after a week's wear you had to force yourself to pick them up and put them on. By day ten, eleven, twelve they would stand up by themselves when you took them off. After a fortnight's hard wear, all day every day, they were finally taken off for a wash and usually they would also have to be darned and you wore your other pair.

Every year a huge shoe bin was pulled out and you scrambled around for a pair of shoes that might fit. The shoes were tied together and the size was written on them. We were told to keep a note in our heads of what size we'd been the year before and find a pair that fitted. But these shoes had been repaired so many times over, they were old and cracked and patched, most of us just looked for a pair that *looked* halfway decent, and if they fitted you as well, that was an extra bonus. We were very hard on our shoes. One of the ways we kept ourselves amused was to tear back and forth in the yard and create sparks from the metal plates on the soles. That soon wore the leather out. When that happened, we used to put a piece of cardboard inside to cover up the hole. If you had wide feet and the shoes just cracked from the strain we did the same thing. If anything happened to the shoes during the year you just had to make do and get on with it. At the end of the year the shoes went off to the cobblers and the cardboard was replaced with patches of leather ready for the next girl. I have had bunions all my life from never being properly fitted for shoes.

There was a time when they introduced glasses for the children. We thought that was great fun – covering up one eye and reading the faraway chart and occasionally getting a letter wrong deliberately just to be one of the lucky ones who were given spectacles. We just wanted something new that hadn't belonged to anyone else and would be our own personal property. Lydia did really well. She got great big thick ones that made her eyes look enormous. I was very envious and determined to get myself a pair by hook or crook. But I didn't just want the cheap ones that were being dished out, I had my sights set on a pair Sister Kevin had in her possession, left to her when one of the nuns had died. She had shown them to us one day. They were genuine tortoiseshell, slim and elegant, and I'd have done anything to get my hands on them. I went to her and said I couldn't read and could I have an eye test like my sister had had. It wasn't an optician, but a doctor. She was a dumpy woman whom I saw only twice in my eight years at Moate. On this occasion I managed to fail on enough points to warrant a pair of glasses. I was so happy; I couldn't believe it had worked. At the end of the test I managed to summon up enough courage to suggest that I had the tortoiseshell ones from her top drawer just to save money. Sister Kevin was no fool, she had clearly seen that one coming a mile off and said, No, those ones were nothing like strong enough for someone with my impaired vision, I would need these, she said, handing me a pair of the biggest, ugliest glasses I had ever seen.

I tried them on and knew I looked like a total gom, an eejit, and that was exactly what the other girls said I was when I made what should have been a triumphant return to the classroom. I wore them initially despite the fact that they didn't flatter me in the slightest and as soon as I could I left them under my bed. Sister Aquin noticed immediately. 'Where are your glasses, Kathleen!'

'I've forgotten them, sister,' I said.

'If you don't come to school with them tomorrow, I'm going to send you down to the orphanage.'

'Yes, sister.'

The scenario was the same the following day; I wasn't giving in easily.

'Go back to the orphanage and get your glasses.'

I went back to the orphanage, which was something you were never, ever allowed to do, and was caught by Sister Kevin in the cloister. 'What are you doing away from school?' she snapped.

'Forgot my glasses, sister,' I replied, and scuttled off to the dorm which was like a different place without all the other girls in it. This went on for weeks, but I wasn't giving in. I was fed up with being called a big gom. I wasn't an eejit and I was not going to be called a great lump. I aspired to looking pretty and glamorous with a wave in my hair and the horn-rimmed specs would have helped no end. But that wasn't going to happen with these glasses. In the end, Sister Aquin gave up; the struggle was just too much.

We received almost no medical attention. You had to be very sick indeed to call a doctor. Once Sarah Louise was beaten very badly right in the middle of the refectory in front of all of us. I just stood there watching her trying to be brave and not cry.

The next day she looked really unwell. She was pale as a ghost, could barely walk to chapel and vomited up her breakfast. The nuns clearly knew that this was serious; there was lots of whispering in the refectory and – whether it was concern for Sarah Louise or themselves – I'd never seen them look so worried. I kept thinking, What will they do if my sister dies and the news gets out about what they did to her? They began to give her daily doses of milk with a raw egg mixed in, in order to build up her strength again. They didn't call a doctor because of the bruises and marks on her body but luckily she slowly got better again, much to the nuns' relief.

I remember being sick one day, and I started hallucinating. I was obviously quite feverish because they'd let me stay in the dormitory instead of going to school as usual. I was lying in bed looking out of the high windows feeling very hot and sweaty, and I saw Jesus on a cross in the sky, with the archangel Gabriel on one side and the Virgin Mary on the other. It was all up there in the cloud formation. I told Miss Carberry and she said, 'You must stop making things up, Kathleen!'

If you ever did get sick enough to land up in the infirmary you could rest and food was brought to you in bed. It was the one place where you were treated better. Once when I was in there the doctor came in to do his rounds and I overheard Sister Bernadette saying when he came down near to our beds, 'Don't bother with them – they're just orphans.' Once again I presumed they were aware that they had to cover up for themselves. We all had chilblains from working outside in the cold, burns from the irons in the laundry room, head lice in our hair and bruises from the beatings – how could they have explained all of those to a medical professional? They would do anything rather than send us to the infirmary where the doctor might visit. Once, my eyes became so sore I could not open them in the mornings because they had become dry and crusted over from the discharge during the nights. The only reaction I got was to be called 'scabby eyes' by the other girls. Eventually I was taken to see a doctor in Athlone who told me that flies had got stuck in my eyes.

Our dental care was no better. Our teeth were pulled out in the kitchen and we were held down by Sister Kevin and Miss Carberry. One of the older girls said it was because when your mouth bled they could just wipe down the kitchen floor. I remember three of us girls sitting on a bench in the kitchen waiting for the man who pulled the teeth to come and speak to us. I was feeling very worried and obviously showed it because when the man asked me where I was from and tried to make a joke, 'Ahhh! You're a dirty Dubliner.' It was supposed to be funny – something to take my mind off the impending pain – but all I could think of was that this stranger thought I was grubby and worthless just as everyone else seemed to.

For most of us there was no respite from the drudgery, no holidays, unlike (once again, to my great envy) the boarding-school girls. The only consolation was that when they had gone home for the summer we were allowed to set foot on their playing field – just once – for our sports day. A few of the girls from the Industrial School also went home for a fortnight in the summer and I started to hope that one year it might be our turn. I asked my sisters if Mammy had said anything to them about us coming home but they just looked at me blankly. Every year when the summer holidays started I prayed that it was going to be us. But two or three years passed and often the same girls went home, nobody ever even seemed to consider us and I started to feel sad and resentful. Why them and not me? I said this one day to one of the big girls who never seemed to go home either and she just looked at me as though I was even more of a gom than she had previously suspected and with a very withering look said, 'The ones that go home have a mother *and* a father, and haven't come from the slums or lived on the streets, eejit!'

If you had both parents you were treated respectfully and if you were in some way related to the nuns you were literally the teachers' pets. There was another family who were treated far better than the rest of us. I could never work out why until one day I discovered from one of the older girls that their father was with the IRA and had been arrested for having ammunition in his home. Well, the nuns certainly knew better than to upset those two girls who had been put in the Industrial School when their daddy went to prison: they were treated with the softest of kid gloves. They became pets because the Sisters of Mercy were frightened of the IRA. Both those sets of girls were the crème de la crème at Moate. They were at the top of our pecking order.

One year, one of the girls who was known as 'Massa' told me she was being allowed home for a holiday; she went on and on about it until I started to loathe her. I couldn't help it: I had to take revenge on someone. This girl came from Athlone and a rumour started that she had been seen riding a dog round the town. This was our ultimate insult and I remember taunting her with it again and again. The more I said it, the more of a vile smelly mongrel that dog became. She got very upset which I was pleased about. We needed only the slightest provocation to turn very nasty to each other.

I never asked the nuns if I was going home because deep down I suspected that it was to do with the bad things I'd done: the things that had got us into Moate in the first place. I still didn't really know what I had done wrong but I knew that we would still be living with Mammy if I hadn't gone to Luke McCabe's room that day. My daydreams of running away had long ceased, though one girl tried and apparently got to Kilcock about thirty-six miles away before she was picked up by a lorry driver who offered her a lift but actually took her to the nearest police station. She was severely flogged. It was meant to be a deterrent to us, but secretly we all admired her bravery. We knew we would never dare emulate her.

Chapter 11

We saw so little of the outside world, we stopped being curious about it. I remember one day though looking out of the small windows of the top dormitory and seeing army trucks full of soldiers going to Athlone in the distance. There were two army barracks in close vicinity to our school – one in Mullingar and one in Athlone – and troops moved regularly between the two. We used to sit on the window sill, and then we were high enough up to look over the six-foot wall surrounding the boarding school as well. Bridie used to say she wished the soldiers would break into Moate and come and kill all the nuns. I would never have dared say anything like that but I too longed for something to vary the unrelenting routine of our lives. The only time it did change was when the nuns went on one of their retreats. Father Jones, of the Redemptorist Order, came into Moate and that was usually the first sign we had that this was about to happen. I never did work out the precise timing of these retreats – perhaps it was Easter or Whitsun – but once a year, the nuns would lock themselves away for a week or ten days and we were left alone with Miss

Carberry or Miss Joyce. Miss Joyce was a teacher who taught the boarders but at this time she took over our classes and she made a pleasant change. We always had to be very quiet during these times, but otherwise the atmosphere was more carefree than it was the rest of the year.

When Miss Carberry and Miss Joyce were left in charge things changed a lot. Miss Carberry would play gramophone records in the workroom next to the refectory. She played country and western, Slim Whitman, music that my mother had played, and it always took me right back to when I was a little girl and made me feel homesick. I don't know where she got the records from – we never saw them the rest of the year – but once the nuns had departed we knew that she could be persuaded to play us some music. We would plead with her and eventually she would give in. Sometimes she even let us dance, as long as we weren't close to each other. Sometimes we would act the fool and drag each other round in a waltz-like manner and she would get quite worked up and say, 'Behave yourselves or you will sit down!' It was an ongoing refrain.

In order to keep out of their way, we did everything in the workroom whilst the nuns were on retreat. We did our home-work, our knitting, our sewing, our praying and our catechism. It was a very large room and in one corner there was a big cabinet where the gramophone was stored when it wasn't in use. There was a desk at the front where the nuns sat when they were there and then there were long benches and desks with inkwells in them in line all the way down the room, where we did our knitting and sewing. We always sat in the same places. We weren't allowed out into the yard during these periods, so breaks were spent inside the workroom sitting on the radiators trying to get warm. We would loll around vacantly and Miss Joyce and Miss Carberry would oversee us. I can't say it was pleasant, but it was more pleasant than what we were used to. It was different and that was a relief in itself.

Then for two weeks in the summer the nuns went away to Spiddal for a holiday. This was the moment when some of the orphans who didn't have 'unsuitable mothers' (as the nuns repeatedly told us we did) were allowed to go home for a fortnight as well. During this fortnight, even though we still had to do manual labour, the atmosphere was a bit more relaxed.

One day a year we too were allowed to go to the seaside. We went by coach to Coosan Point and it was a great, great treat. We made egg sandwiches and jam sandwiches and took big bottles of orangeade and it seemed the most wonderful thing ever. Sitting on the beach, eating that delicious food made me think of Mammy and all the lovely times we had together at the beach with my friend Chrissie Dumphy and all the other local kids.

We were each given a swimming costume for the day of our outing. These were made of some sort of elasticated fabric with a smocking front and baggy bottoms – one size fitted all. Despite the fact that they were a bit musty and didn't fit us very well in places, we ran around in them just happy to be away from school and feeling the sea air on our faces. We were so excited; it was a day's holiday and we wanted it to go on for ever. And the nuns were always nice to us because it was a public place and they were aware how much they were on show. Though it wasn't exactly crowded – we didn't go to the bit of the beach which everyone else went to. I don't know if it was for modesty's sake or privacy but we always walked to the far end of the shingly beach where no one else went. Sister Kevin and the other nuns used to tuck the bottom of their habits up underneath their belts, still leaving plenty of fabric to cover their knees and legs. For one day of the year, no one shouted at us and we had a grand old time.

Once during the summer Miss Carberry went into the town

and bought a block of ice cream. She cut it into thin slivers and placed them between wafers; she could make one little block go round forty odd girls quite easily, she boasted. She handed the little ice cream sandwiches out of the big open window of St Martha's, the room where the cooking was done and the bread was kept, and even though it was thin and melting faster than you could eat it, it tasted like heaven.

The only other break in our routine was the arrival of a letter or a present from Mammy. She never forgot Easter or Christmas and when it was your birthday there was always a parcel with something in it for the others as well. This was one bit of our welfare which she could contribute to and she never let us down once. Sometimes we were allowed to write back but it was made very clear that our letters would be read for content before they were sent. They were also only posted as and when the nuns saw fit, which often bore little relation to when they had actually been written. Postage stamps were expensive, after all, and the general feeling was they were wasted on the pathetic little scribblings of orphans. I only found this out after I left and questioned Mammy about the long delays between my letters going out and her replies coming back. But really the whole thing was nonsense. We were told what to put into the letters and we knew we would be given a beating if we didn't put in what they wanted us to. Generally my letters went along these lines: *My dear mammy, I hope you are well. I am very well thank you. Thank you for your lovely present. I'm having a lovely time. I'm very happy here. I remain your loving daughter, Kathleen.*

I knew better than to put down my real feelings, so I just put in what I knew was safe to get past the nuns. And I became very mercenary. I wasn't allowed to tell Mammy the truth or ask her about her life so I just said please send this, please send that and in due course those things would arrive.

Mammy's letters were similarly straightforward. They just said she was sending us what we'd asked for. She didn't say that she had had another baby or had moved house. They were very basic letters – one page only – and ours were as well. I remember her sending me some Basildon Bond writing paper and envelopes that I had asked for which I loved. I guarded my little writing set with my life, never lent it out and got Miss Carberry to look after it at the end of the day. Thieving was rife at the Industrial School and if you had something nice you had to protect it, or it would go 'missing'. Mammy once sent me some pretty embroidered handkerchiefs and rather than leave them hanging around after washing them, I put them between the mattress and the metal springs of the bed. At least that way they were dry, flat and most importantly safe. My other few possessions I also gave to Miss Carberry for safe-keeping. Effectively, you never got to own anything at Moate, as you had nowhere to keep it safe. We had a few more posses-sions than other people because Mammy never forgot us. I knew we were lucky because some of the girls never got anything and they always looked with such envy at Mammy's big parcels all tied up in brown paper and string.

One year Mammy sent me a skipping rope which I loved. Suddenly I was very popular – everyone wanted to do skipping with me out in the yard. We called each other names as we were doing it: Bridie was purple legs, purple legs. I was stumps of trees, stumps of trees. We had to find some defect in each other and exploit it. Every day we played with it and every night I gave it to Winnie Carberry.

One day Bridie came running up to me in the cloisters and said, 'Your mammy's just come into the yard and she's got a little baby with her. It's a little boy dressed in blue!' She was so excited for me; we both loved babies and, being wholly igno-rant of the facts of life, felt how kind it was of Mammy to bring in a real baby for us to see. Wasn't God good giving Mammy another baby! After all, the nuns kept praying for more children and now Mammy had got another one! We were so excited.

Bridie was swiftly followed by Sister Kevin who announced in her rather condescending way that, 'Your mother has turned up,' as though she had just wafted in there like a bad smell. I heard the insult, but I wasn't going to let her get to me on this of all days.

'Mammy's got a new baby,' I said to Sarah Louise and Lydia who looked wide-eyed with pleasure too. We quickly put on our smart clothes and rushed down to see her. She was as neat as ever in her carefully pressed suit and she had Paul on one side, who was a proper toddler now, and the little baby (my half-brother as I later realised) nestled against her in a white crocheted blanket. As soon as he saw us, he started gurgling and making such funny faces we began to laugh and play with him. Mammy wasn't on her own. Paddy McNamara, the man we used to play with at the beach, was there and he seemed to give her the confidence she needed to face the nuns. We sat outside on the bench in the yard, and the presence of the baby made it much more relaxed and easier to chat than the last time she'd come in. Everyone was looking at us, which I loved; the other children stared openly and clusters of nuns kept coming out to have a look at this man on our mother's arm. But Mammy wasn't being over-deferential on this occasion. She knew the nuns looked down on her but now she had Paddy McNamara with her, it clearly gave her the respect she had previously been lacking.

It was a year since I'd last seen her and I still assumed that she was living at Lower Bridge Street and everything was just as it had been, frozen in time. In fact she had moved once we had been taken from her; living above Georgina McCabe and all those bad memories was just too hard to bear. But she didn't mention that during our short time together; she didn't want to disturb the status quo at all.

So much had happened since we had last seen her; we had known nothing of the arrival of the new baby and she in turn knew nothing of our daily lives: the scrubbing and the daily punishments and the fact that we were only ever together again – as sisters – when she came to visit. We didn't tell her that we cried in bed most nights and that we wet the bed again now, we just fussed over the baby, who was called Bill, and enjoyed the nice warm feeling of sitting next to Mammy on the bench, playing with Paul and holding the baby's tiny hands in ours. The feeling of belonging to a family again was wonderful. The other children formed a sort of makeshift circle around us and I felt so important. Then, almost as soon as she had come, it was time for Mammy to go and one of the nuns came to escort her out of the yard. But we still had the sweets and the spinning tops that she had given us and the girls continued to crowd around us asking if they could mind them for us or if they could have a lick. Then it was all over, the circle disappeared and the old familiar feeling of emptiness rose inside me again. Mammy had travelled all the way to see us and they never once offered her a cup of tea or a glass of water.

I don't remember anyone else having a visitor except us. Mammy was allowed to visit once a year in the summer and as far as I was concerned that was the one and only time the outside world came into the convent. Sometimes I wonder how I became so blinkered, so buried in my own problems that I failed to see other people coming and going. I now know that quite a few parents and relatives visited and they weren't restricted to just once a year as my mother was. My mother was under strict instruction that she could *only* visit once a year, but parents and relatives whose faces fitted came in a couple of times and even during termtime when they might be seen by the boarders and the Technical-School pupils. Perhaps I chose not to see their comings and goings; it was easier to think of us all alone and friendless: the orphans that the school pretended we were.

Quite soon after Mammy's visit I bumped into Sister Cecilia on my way to do the laundry or some such chore. We were never allowed to look at the nuns directly in the eye. When we passed, we had to stand stock still and cast our eyes down and just say, 'Hello, Sister Cecilia.' But there was this one occasion – a vivid one – when she stopped me and said, 'Your mother, never mind, dear . . . She causes a lot of trouble. She can't help it. Whenever she telephones or visits she always makes a scene. Anyone would think she hadn't seen girls with properly clipped hair before! Or that we were personally to blame for those head lice you've all got.'

I guessed she was referring to my mother's visit a few weeks before but exactly what Mammy had done wrong was a bit of a mystery. I kept my eyes down and felt ashamed that my family was causing trouble, and just said, 'Yes, sister.' Maybe she realised from my downcast face that it had hurt the way it was meant to hurt because suddenly she did something she'd never done before. She put her hand into the deep pocket of her habit and pulled out a rather hairy-looking, squashed chocolate and gave it to me. I couldn't believe it. Although Sister Monica occasionally gave me a sweet in the ironing room, it was never a chocolate one. Even though it was filthy, it still tasted lovely; and even though I felt like Judas because a minute before she had been speaking badly about my mother, I ate it – and it was worth it.

I knew little of what this 'fuss' was about but I knew there was great tension whenever my mother came in. She didn't want us to be there. She could see that we were in poor health and badly treated and she did question them about it and they didn't like that. Despite the sisters' protestations she could tell with her mother's instinct that we were not the children who had been living with her. She tried to put on a good front when she saw us, and we tried to put on a good front when we saw her, but I'm not sure who was really kidding whom.

There was great excitement one day when it was announced that the new sewing room, which had been built on to one side of the workroom, was finished and ready for us. It contained five Singer pedal machines and was where we would do all our sewing and repairs. We thought it was very impressive, very up-to-the-minute and we always referred to it as the New Sewing Room with a great deal of reverence in our voices. We used to repair the old sheets in there, sheets which had been passed down to us from the convent and boarding school. We cut them down the centre then sewed outside edge to outside edge to make a new one. We used to do hedge tears on minor rips by sewing them over and over again and on big holes we used to sew patches. It was an endless job and there was little satisfaction in it because you knew that every seam you put on them just made them even scratchier and lumpier and more uncomfortable than they were already.

Mammy was always pleased to hear that we had been sewing because it was something she liked. The nuns were really very clever with a needle; they were famous for it. They used to embroider the vestments for the priests and some of those were breathtakingly fine and delicate. We too were expected to acquire a wide range of needlework skills from sewing and mending to knitting and darning. We were also expected to learn the art of embroidery, not for our own pleasure, but for sale. I remember one year I made a cushion cover with dahlias embroidered on it and I was so pleased with it, I wanted to send this cushion home to Mammy as a present to show her what I could do. A lot of our sewing and knitting was put into the sale of work in the town; I told Sister Bernard that I wanted to buy the cushion cover and she told me the price, which was the same they would have charged if they had put it into the sale. They were doing me a great turn, they said, they could have sold it for even more at Clery's! and they came up with a sum which was far too much considering I'd done all the work in the first place. However, with the money that Mammy had sent to me over time, I bought her the cushion.

It seems such a crime to me now that they made us buy back work we had done but that was what we did. They earned out of us – it was a workhouse and this just rammed that fact home. But at the time I didn't question it. When you've been told for years that, 'We picked you out of the gutters of Dublin and gave you a roof over your head,' you stop questioning anything. Years later, when I went home, Mammy still had that cushion, it had pride of place on her favourite armchair. She kept it for years and years until she died.

'It was a grand day when that arrived in the post, Kathleen,' she used to say. I was so happy to see how much she treasured it. There was so little I could give back to her.

Over the years Mammy sent us a whole variety of gifts: things we needed like handkerchiefs and clips for our hair, pencils, items that would have been a normal part of childhood but which were not a normal part of life in the Industrial School. And if we asked for a particular article she went out of her way to find the best quality she could. It was fashionable at the time to have a pen and pencil set in a leather case with a flap to keep everything neat. Sarah Louise had received one the previous year which I had coveted and told Mammy so in a letter; when it came to my birthday she sent me one in lovely black leather with smart stitching.

We were sent presents and the other girls generally weren't – or not as frequently – and that caused some resentment. And I was fiercely possessive of anything I did receive. I remember on one of her visits, Mammy brought a lovely cake from one of the bakers in Dublin and the lay teacher Miss Joyce, who occasionally supervised us in the refectory, made me share that cake with all the other girls on the table. I remember feeling really cross. They never shared their cake with me because they never got any so why should I share mine? What was mine was mine and no one should be allowed to touch it.

On the Feast Days of the nuns with whom we were directly involved, we would be given a piece of cake or a biscuit, or we were allowed off homework – but on *our* birthdays there was nothing. We were never allowed to feel like individuals and certainly never allowed to feel special or significant. We had nothing to celebrate. The school ignored our birthdays entirely but Mammy never did. One year when I was about thirteen I decided that what I wanted more than anything else in the world was a new doll. When we'd been taken away by the courts, we had only what we stood up in and I had missed the dolls and prams I used to have as a little girl so much over the years; it made me sad just thinking about them. I was really too grown up for such things now but I decided to ask Mammy to send me one anyway. She had written to us recently to say that she had moved to England and we could have a special present – what would we like? I asked Lydia what she was asking for and she said – whether it was to copy me or not I don't know – she wanted a dolly too.

Mine arrived first. It was exquisite. It had a beautiful face, blond hair and a lovely old-fashioned-looking pink taffeta dress with matching bonnet and booties. I loved it so much; I couldn't believe Mammy had bought me such a gorgeous dolly – it must have cost a fortune. I was so happy with that doll; at long last I had something of my own to play with again. But my happiness was brought to a sudden halt by Sarah Louise coming to me, prompted by Sister Kevin, to say I had to give it to Lydia because hers hadn't arrived and it wasn't fair that I should have one and she didn't. Sister Kevin then said, 'Lydia's younger than you. She believes in Father Christmas. And you'll get it back when her doll arrives because you know your mammy will send it – she always does.'

'No,' I said, 'I'm not giving away that doll; that doll is mine.' Although I was quite scared of my big sister and very scared of Sister Kevin I remember pursing my lips and just shaking my head. 'No.' I would not back down and give that doll to Lydia or anyone. She was mine and Mammy had sent it to me. I felt guilty about Lydia, but I just couldn't stop myself.

In the end Lydia's doll arrived just before Christmas and everything was all right. We both had our dolls to play with at last. But I never let that doll out of my sight. I loved her fiercely and never allowed anyone else to touch her. I never undressed her or changed her hairstyle or anything. She was still immaculate and untouched when I was well into my thirties.

If Mammy's thoughtfulness never wavered as the years passed, neither did the other constant of school life: the beatings. They are my over-riding memory of Moate. They went on continually and wore you down completely. After a year or so in, I had come to accept them just as you accepted that you got up every morning and said your prayers: it was part of life. Sometimes one of the big girls was put in charge of us for a few minutes when one of the nuns had to leave the room. At first I was pleased when I saw this happening, I thought it would be an improvement but it wasn't. The older girl would just take the opportunity to pick on whoever had been bothering her and hit and punish her. One time it happened to me and I just saw red. I shouted at her, 'Don't think you can boss me around. You're just another orphan.' She still whacked me for it but later when I saw her being punished for something else, I took more than a bit of pleasure in it.

I had learnt very soon that the only defence we had was not letting the nuns have the satisfaction of seeing us cry. After a beating you'd come back and say defiantly, 'She didn't make me cry.' You fought the tears very hard so that no one ever saw them. I discovered that if you had been hit on your hands you could make the pain go away by putting them under your armpits and pressing your arms hard against your body. The tears I held over until night-time and cried to myself under the blanket. All the girls dealt with their own situations, their own pain, in private. There was no sharing or communication. Occasionally someone got really upset and then we would take the risk of putting our arms around them, but it was rare; you knew you ran the risk of getting the same beating so it made you very cautious.

Ironically, given this lack of companionship and the loneliness it ensured, we were never allowed to be by ourselves, not even when we wanted to go to the toilet. When the last call went out at eight in the evening that the toilet was to be closed, we all rushed out of bed and queued up on the stairs. Sometimes if you only wanted to pee or just couldn't hang on any longer, you'd jump the queue saying, 'I'll be quick. Can I go in front of you or I'll just go out through the leg of my knickers.' Whether you'd queued up or otherwise, all the time you were doing what you needed to do, Winnie Carberry would be standing in the doorway keeping an eye on you, checking that you weren't up to any mischief or touching yourself. She stood in the doorway knitting, resting on one leg, with the other shorter leg crossed over it, checking we weren't up to the devil's work.

That was it then: bed and sleep. But the big girls were allowed to sit up and knit. All of their beds were together under the one light, and so they would all sit up in their beds doing their knitting under the watchful eyes of Miss Carberry or Sister Bernadette. There was no light where the little ones slept so they just had to get under the covers and close their eyes. There was no talking, or laughing, just silence except for the clack,

clack, clack of the big girls' knitting needles. If you behaved badly then the punishment was to be sent to the end of the dormitory where the little ones were, in the dark.

Another punishment that was meted out at night-time if you were caught being disobedient was that you had to carry your mattress out to the landing and sleep there alongside the statue of the Virgin Mary whose stony presence towered over you on her large plinth. I spent many a night out there and still have nightmares about it more than fifty years later. Rumour was that it was haunted and since there was only ever one girl at a time out there, it was a very frightening place to be. The moon cast big, bright, fleeting shadows like ghosts across the ceiling and walls. I remember hearing every clank, clank of the noisy central heating system which we had taunted each other was actually the sound of the rats running through the radiator pipes. Suddenly, when you were lying there all by yourself, you could clearly hear their sharp feet as they pattered by near your head. And there were mice everywhere scuttling about near between their various holes nearby. I tried to drop off and not think about the filthy smelly things running around me but it was quite terrifying. Then just as I was about to sink into sleep another shadow would come through the window willing me to open my eyes. The landing was small, not much bigger than twice the size of the mattress, and what struck you was how alone you were: it was the loneliness which got to you almost as much as the fear.

Once, in the middle of the night, when we were all asleep in our beds, a fire broke out downstairs. We didn't know what had happened, we just woke up to a lot of raised voices and a strange bitter smell. Still bleary-eyed from sleep we were ushered out of the dormitory and down to St Joseph's Hall, in our bare feet and nightdresses. The smell was even stronger down there. It was very noisy, the little girls were crying from having been woken up but I felt a bit excited that something out of the norm was happening. I remember hearing the never-to-be-repeated sound of nuns running in the corridors and that seemed extraordinary to me. We still had no idea what was happening until the Reverend Mother said flatly, as though it was a regular occurrence, 'There was a fire. It's been put out. You may all go back to your beds now.' Then she added, almost as an afterthought, 'You must not breathe a word of this to anyone. If anyone mentions it in the school they will be for it.' I knew what that meant – a public flogging – and went quietly up to bed along with the rest of the girls. But in the days that followed the story did get out. Sarah Louise told one of the National-School girls whom she saw in the classroom what had happened and this girl came straight out and said to the nun in charge of the class, 'Was there a fire in the middle of the night?' The nuns were so furious to have been disobeyed, we were rounded up in the yard in the cold and told we had to stand until whoever had told owned up. My sister never did confess, so we were all punished. We had to stand up for every meal in the refectory for a week.

The fire was a one-off; a sound I would often hear at night was Miss Carberry crying to herself. She tried to stifle it but even with the partition you could hear it. It was always particularly bad when Sister Kevin had given her a public dressing down. I was at Moate School for eight years in total and most of those nights I heard that woman sob herself to sleep. It didn't surprise me when someone told me that Miss Carberry had been an orphan there herself and had just never left. You couldn't get much past her because she, of all people, really did know what was going on. She had a horrible life. She had never known anything except that place. If she didn't give us a hard time, Kevin would give her a hard time; she was abused by Kevin and so she was abusive to us and we hated her and were mean to her whenever we got the chance. Her bad hip and short leg made her a very easy target for abuse.

Whenever we felt we had been unjustly treated – beaten unnecessarily – we used to take the mickey out of her and call her 'hopalong' under our breath. We used to say that she'd had an accident riding a dog, not a horse, because that seemed more demeaning. It was pointless and cruel, but then so was our life in Moate.

Chapter 12

Amidst the gloom one positive and happy event at Moate occurred when there was a big choir competition in Athlone. All the schools in the surrounding areas were eligible and even we – the orphans – were allowed to enter. For once we were going to mix with the other girls. Suddenly we were given blazers, new green jumpers and a type of gymslip which looked a bit like the lovely pleated ones that the boarding-school girls wore. They were new and it was the first time in about five years that we'd been given clothes which weren't on their last legs. We suspected something was going on but we didn't mind. 'Aren't the nuns great!' we said to each other the day they were dished out. 'Aren't the clothes gorgeous!' We were all dressed up and couldn't really believe how our luck had changed. I remember walking around Athlone on the competition day, cock-a-hoop in my new outfit. We had even been given new ankle socks to go with our new brown sandals, which we were then allowed to wear every Sunday. The last time I'd had so many new things was when Mammy took me shopping for my Holy Communion. The competition came round and we sang our hearts out but we didn't win, which was very disappointing. Later when we got back I asked Miss Carberry for my writing paper and wrote a long excited letter to Mammy all about the new outfit, the lovely day and the competition that we should have won and didn't.

I loved singing. We'd been taught to sing the Mass in Latin and to me it was the most beautiful sound I had ever heard. If I closed my eyes and focused on those angelic voices, I was transported to another more heavenly place. I wanted to be as close to that sound as I could be so tried very hard and managed to get into the choir. Mammy had always told me I had a lovely voice and now was my chance to show it. It was a simple choir – we didn't have altos or sopranos, we just had firsts, seconds and thirds, and naturally we were all expected to stick to our parts. One day though I was up in the Gods, singing with the seconds – Sister Cecilia was playing the organ and it was magical, a lovely sound – when I noticed that the firsts were sounding a bit weak and thin. I decided that they needed help, so I moved over – not physically but tonally; I began singing the first part. I can still see Sister Magdalene's stunned, angry face. She couldn't pinpoint who it was but she could clearly hear that someone was doing something she hadn't instructed them to. She couldn't correct me because we sang this Mass every Sunday for the public; we had to be dignified. It didn't occur to me that I might get a beating, all I could think about was that the firsts needed my help. I wasn't upsetting anything, I was putting it right.

There was a pecking order among the nuns when they attended chapel. The Reverend Mother and Mother Malachy, the assistant Reverend Mother had their own throne-like, individual pews, right at the back of the chapel, facing the altar as befitted their status at the top of the ladder. Close by them in an especially reserved pew along the side of the chapel were the more senior nuns. Behind them were the lay nuns in benches where they prayed and the novices were at the front in pews. We sat in a little extension to the left of the nuns' chapel but you could see quite clearly down into their chapel.

We sang the Mass and Benediction for the public on a Sunday in Moate parish church and we attended a second Benediction later in the day in the nuns' own chapel. So we had two Masses and two Benedictions on a Sunday and every fortnight we went to confession. But I could rarely think of anything to confess to. Mammy had taught me what was wrong and what was right and we never had a chance to do any of the bad things she had mentioned, so what was there to say? In time though the nuns instilled a very strong sense of guilt in me and I could reel off a list of crimes at the drop of a hat: 'I told a lie, Father', 'I had a bad thought', 'I was wicked to my sister'. The more sins I managed to admit to the more the priest seemed pleased with me: I was just given a few hail Marys, 'Don't do it again my child,' and sent off into the world hopefully to commit a few more so that we could go through the same process in two weeks' time.

In due course confession became a game. I knew you had to go in order to have a clean soul to receive Holy Communion. We went every fortnight which was – ironically – as often as we changed our knickers. We knew that we had to come up with something because then we could receive Holy Communion on the Sunday. And I was determined to be a good girl. I knew I had committed a mortal sin because I had let Luke McCabe do dirty things to me. I would have done anything to cleanse my soul. I was happy to fast along with the other girls in order to be prepared for my Sunday treat. Even if I felt a bit weak and faint from lack of food I always eagerly awaited the Body of Christ in the form of that wafer. If anything could make me holy, that could, I thought as I swallowed it, trying not to chew it a bit before it went down . . . but it did have a nice taste and sometimes I would have the tiniest nibble as it went down.

I knew you weren't allowed to but sometimes it was just too tempting.

We lived more or less entirely in a world of females. The two men we saw on a regular basis were Canon Pinkman, who ran the parish, and Father McKeon, the priest who said the daily Mass. Canon Pinkman and Father McKeon lived together in a nice big house inside the parish church grounds a five-minute walk from us. They shared a housekeeper called Mary Ward and she sometimes used to take pity on us and give us her scraps from the kitchen. She used to say we looked like scraps ourselves. Father McKeon was a lovely man, very handsome. Sister Aquin's job was to look after the vestry and his vestments and it was quite clear to us girls that she liked him quite a lot. She was petite and very pretty herself and with my over-active imagination, I decided they would go rather well together.

When I was twelve I was told that I must prepare for my Confirmation. I immediately wrote to Mammy telling her the exciting news and asking if I could have a missal of my very own. She wrote back saying she was very happy I was going to be confirmed, and enclosed a beautiful black leather-bound missal. I loved that book. It contained the Gospels, the Mass and the Benediction and was in Latin and English. I used to take it with me every Sunday when I went to Mass. Father McKeon would say and we would sing the Mass in Latin, and I would follow it in English in my missal. After Mass each Sunday I would give it back to Miss Carberry until the following week. Mammy was not invited to my confirmation.

Just as the nuns had chosen their Feast Days from a list of Saint's Days, so in preparation for our Confirmation we were allowed to choose a name which appealed to us for our religious coming-of-age. Although I knew this was an additional name rather than a replacement name, to me this was marvellous. At last I had a chance to get an attractive, sophisticated name like my sisters. I was so bored with Kathleen. Half of Ireland had the same name and I desperately longed to be different. There was even a pop song – 'I'll take you home again, Kathleen' – and I thought I could do so much better. Sister Malachy read out the list and the first name I heard that I liked was Jacinta. One of the three girls at Fatima we had been hearing about was called that and it had always struck me as very pretty and feminine. Then I heard it, the name I had been waiting for: *Attracta*. I don't know why, but something clicked at that moment. It sounded so gorgeous, I decided to take it as my saint's name. But when I tried to find out about her from the nuns I just drew a blank. The nuns had emphasised the need to take a name because of the *virtues* of that particular saint and I lived in dread of being asked about her and not being able to answer. But no one knew anything about her. They thought she might have been a martyr but no one was quite sure. I was terrified that in the middle of my Confirmation the Bishop would stop and ask me to tell him about St Attracta and then he would refuse to go through with my Confirmation after all.

I had no idea I was illegitimate until I was confirmed. I didn't even know what the word meant. The majority of the girls who were being confirmed had their birth certificates which obviously gave details of both their parents. I did not have my certificate which gave me reason to wonder a bit; I just had my baptismal certificate which only had Mammy's name on it. In fact it was the very absence of a piece of paper which made me realise that I was different. I looked at the other girls' certificates and realised that both their parents had the same name because they were married to each other. I knew that my father's would have been different to my mother's and I started to put two and two together. Although I didn't really know the full meaning of the word illegitimate, I knew it wasn't a very nice word and I was beginning to suspect it might apply to me.

I remember the Confirmation day itself very well. I was standing in the yard waiting to go over to the parish church. There was great excitement all around me, but I felt different. I felt a great sense of shame and embarrassment which I had never experienced before. It was about Mammy and where I had come from and many things I hadn't questioned before. I had no idea who my daddy was. It had never mattered before, but now it mattered deeply, painfully, right inside me. I did my best to hide it but even on a day like that which should have been a celebration, there was something forcing me back into my shell. I stood in that line clutching my beautiful missal but the other girls had a document in their hands which confirmed their mammy's name and their daddy's name. On this as on so many days of my life, I lived in terror of being found out.

Physically I was growing up, but I was still a very confused child. I yearned to be as pure as the nuns were: their virginal habits and clean, pure, visionary faces. The more I looked at them, the more I didn't want to be me. I didn't like the way the big girls, the fourteen- and fifteen-year-olds looked at Father McKeon or the men we sometimes saw out in the far fields.

We were given no sex education whatsoever. I knew nothing about monthly periods. I started to notice, though, that some of the girls in the lavatory had blood on their knickers and that seemed to me dirty and something to be ashamed of. We used to call them rude names under our breath and after a while I used to consciously look for it in order to pick on someone and accuse them of being dirty. 'You've soiled your knickers! You're a dirty gur-url.'

Every fortnight when we washed our knickers I was usually next to Maureen Slevin whom I looked up to no end because she was so pretty let me copy her homework. I wanted her to be my special friend but she treated me in the same way as she did the other girls. One day when I was on the first basin and she was on the second, I decided to get back at her. I said to her, 'Your knickers were soiled last night. I saw them in the lavatory – they had stains on them!'

Maureen was unruffled, she just answered softly, 'Quite normal stains,' and suddenly I didn't know what to say; it was the worst insult I could think of and she had chosen not to be ruffled or embarrassed about it. I was very puzzled by the whole thing.

Then I too got the 'normal stains' when I was fourteen years old. I went to the toilet and there it was: the tell-tale blood in my pants. I just felt horrified by the smell and the mess and wondered how on earth I was going to get them clean before someone else saw. Then I remembered something Maureen had said when we were doing the washing. 'When it happens you've got to go and see Sister Kevin.' I decided that this must be the 'it' that she had so puzzlingly referred to and went to see Sister Kevin, feeling very awkward and strange. She immediately announced that it was 'my period' – that was all the explanation I got – and that I should come with her to the cupboard outside the refectory. She gave me a thin, pink belt with safety pins and three sanitary towels which *had to last me*, she said emphatically. There were no more If I Ran Out. Was that clear? She also gave me a small cubicle where I could keep my sanitary belt and any other belongings I wished to. She kept hold of the key at all times so everything was perfectly safe in there. I felt as though I had entered a whole new world of big girls' mysteries and although the cubicle was a real treat – a place at long last to keep my doll and my precious possessions – the rest of it just felt rather confusing. In the toilet I fumbled awkwardly to put the belt on as instructed and went on my way no wiser about what was happening to me and how long it would last. And I was very conscious of the pad.

When I told one of the older girls about it, she said I'd been lucky to get three towels out of the notoriously stingy Sister Kevin. 'Don't expect special treatment again,' she said ominously. Sometimes she only gave you one – two if you were lucky – and you had to wear them until they were hard and dried and filthy. I hated the way I smelt so much during my period and I often used to sneak into the big lavatory to give my pants a wash midway through, putting them under my mattress at night in a futile attempt to dry them. In due course I came to hate those times of the month, the trip to see Sister Kevin for the key to the cupboard, the way you stank after days using the same pad without bathing. As we all menstruated at different times, there was a permanent odour of old dried blood.

Puberty came as a shock to me. Either I didn't register the small bodily changes or I did my best to block them out. I certainly did not welcome the growing evidence of my femininity. I hated it when my breasts started growing. I hated the way they were pointing outwards rather than remaining flat as they had before. Mind you, the nuns did their best as well to ensure they remained hidden; they certainly colluded with me in denying my body its changes. They made us all wear stays which we made ourselves out of stiff calico material. They were interlined so that they were completely solid. They were like a corset, designed to keep breasts entirely out of view. It was modesty at all costs for the nuns and girls alike; they couldn't bear to see large breasts bouncing around when we were playing in the yard. Those stays were the only garment we wore which I had any sort of fondness for. Even when I grew too big for mine I kept hold of it, determined to keep myself as flat as flat could be. The metal buttons were always popping but I managed to get hold of some large safety pins to hold it together. I desperately wanted to stay how I was as a child. That way there was still a chance that I would go back and live with Mammy and everything would be as it once was. But every day there were changes and those changes filled me with horror. One day when I was having my fortnightly bath, I washed myself as I always did, when suddenly I noticed that the lips of my vagina were getting thicker and fuller. My vagina looked so large and ugly to me compared to how I had looked as a little girl, I decided I would like to cut the labia to make them look tidy again. I didn't want to hurt myself, to self-harm, but to get rid of the uneven bits, to make myself flat and neat again. I considered getting the scissors from the new sewing room, then I suddenly had a vivid picture of the blood everywhere and decided against it.

There was no one I could talk to. I didn't know it then but we were all desperately in need of a mother at this time. Instead of which our growing bodies were met with despair and repugnance as though they were the product of our own wilful imaginations. Around this time Sarah Louise told me that one of the nuns had tried to kiss her – properly – on the lips. She had pounced on her. Another girl who had big breasts had said that the nun always came in when she had a bath. Although I hated that nun I didn't like Sarah Louise polluting my mind by saying such a thing about her. The nuns treated us badly but to me they were still holy people and wouldn't do a sinful thing like that. 'She's married to Christ!' I shouted at her. I was so naive and so furious all at the same time.

We were taught nothing about the real world. Instead we were taught rituals: we didn't need to know any more. There was a font on the landing outside the classrooms which contained holy water and we all used to bless ourselves before we entered. Then we would say a prayer. And it clearly worked because I had warts on my hands and they disappeared because of the holy water. Oh yes! I would dip my middle finger into the font, bless myself and any water that was left I would rub into the wart and it did go eventually. It seemed like a miracle at the time. More likely it was the raw potatoes, which were the other way we were told to get rid of warts, and I had access to plenty of those!

So we said a prayer to start the class and at the end we would bless ourselves again. The nuns would say something along the lines of cleanliness is next to godliness and I used to go along with that just like everything else they said. Sometimes a small nagging voice inside me would say, But we don't wash ourselves properly or very often . . . But I guessed she was talking about our insides, our souls, and I knew that mine probably needed more cleansing than most.

The one fixed point in our lives was the certainty of the existence of God. Everything we did and everything the nuns did was in His name. Indeed the reason we were at Mount Carmel in the first place, we were told, was in order to become worthy of Him. We were told this simple truth every day and every day my faith in Him grew stronger.

If we couldn't believe our luck at being allowed to enter the choir competition, we were practically speechless when we were told we were going to stage a play, *Connor the Bard*, and a concert and be given new clothes. We'd had so little entertainment at the school it seemed incredible that we were going to be given the chance to perform not once, but twice, in six months. And Sister Aquin was going to be in charge.

As part of our preparation for the show we had drill with marching to music. It was military-style band music and an outside PE instructor was brought in to teach us a routine. I loved marching up and down; I was thrilled that secular music had come back into my life and it brought back memories of dancing and singing with Mammy. Even more excitingly Sister Aquin proposed that Sarah Louise and I could do the Irish dancing that we had often talked about. We could do a hornpipe or a jig, whatever we chose. We were both hugely excited at the chance, but because we hadn't danced for such a long time, it all went wrong. She was doing one step and I was doing another; she was telling me I was an eejit and I was telling her that she was an eejit. We hardly ever spoke to each other normally and suddenly when we were asked to do something together the old tensions came to the surface again. We couldn't agree and so the dance was stopped; no one was going to waste any time showing us the right way.

Sister Aquin had been given funds for the show and she decided to get us some harmonicas and start up a band teaching us to play by numbers. It was slow progress and ages before we could play what anyone else would recognise as a song. In the end I remember we rather proudly mastered a popular hymn of the time, 'At the end of the day, Just kneel and pray'. Sister Aquin also arranged for us orphans to have elocution lessons – we learnt obvious rhymes like 'How Now Brown Cow' and 'The Rain in Spain Stays Mainly on the Plain' and a rather more curious one which went – 'Timothy Dan was a funny wee man and kept all his wealth in his pockets.'

Sarah Louise, who had bags of confidence, had the lead role in *Connor the Bard* and – even more desirably as far as I was concerned – a part in the doll dance. I had seen them in rehearsals and fell in love immediately with the coy, feminine gestures and the beautiful dresses they were going to be wearing; I longed to be in it and I made it very obvious that I would have given my right arm to be chosen but the line-up had already been decided: and joining Sarah Louise were her friend Mary and another girl called Maria. Then suddenly opportunity knocked – Mary had done something very bad like answering back and Sister Bernadette decided that her punishment was to be taken out of the doll dance. I couldn't believe my ears when I heard that I was to take her place. I was over the moon. I learnt the steps in no time, I was so proud I was going to be doing the doll dance with everyone watching me. It didn't matter at all that I hadn't been their first choice.

Then Sister Aquin did something which was disastrous for

me. In front of all of us she asked Sister Bernadette to let Mary back into the doll dance. Her appeal worked. I was completely devastated. I was so sure I had what it took to be a star in the doll dance and then the chance was taken away from me. I cried and cried. I shouted at Mary that she was a pet. 'It should have been me. It isn't fair.'

Sister Aquin just said, 'That's the end of it – be quiet.' Even though I was dancing in the Sailors' Hornpipe it just wasn't the same, it was silly and childish and, more to the point, I didn't like the horrible boys' clothes we had to wear.

The day of the show arrived; the whole school was very excited. It took place on the rostrum in the National School and they'd made it look really grand with proper chairs laid out and everything. We played our harmonicas and did our marching and our dancing and after we'd finished our bit we were allowed to sit in the audience and watch the rest of the concert. I remember it was full of people in lovely clothes. They all seemed to be watching the show very enthusiastically and whispering to each other behind their hands. I remember being rather amazed. I had thought the audience would be people connected to the school or perhaps the nuns' families. Instead it was full of people who spoke like they did in the movies I had been to see with Mammy. I overheard Sister Bernadette saying at one stage, 'No, their mother won't let them, won't give them up,' but didn't understand what she meant. What I didn't know, but which came out later and spread like wildfire round the yard, was that these American visitors were casting their eyes over the children with a view to paying the nuns to adopt them. The concert was a sort of showcase for them to pick and choose. What we'd thought was a bit of fun playing in the band and learning new skills was actually the nuns grooming us like performing monkeys in a zoo.

Generally the girls who had played the most active roles in the show were 'chosen'. Some of the girls disappeared after that concert and we never saw them again. I hope they went to good families and had a better life than they had in Moate. One of the older girls dared to ask about the American families and was told 'they were good people'. But that could simply have meant they were rich and that was all that mattered.

The play was over; the PE sessions ended, the dancing stopped and even the harmonica lessons which Sister Aquin tried to keep going were brought to an abrupt halt. The play had performed its function and suddenly we were wrenched back to the dismal normality of our lives. Sarah Louise had been the star of the show but she was soon out of favour and getting into trouble and getting flogged again. Even Sister Aquin couldn't help her when she spoke out about what happened in the dormitories at night.

There was an unspoken hierarchy among the girls: the big girls ruled the little girls and if you didn't do what they wanted they bullied you. This was particularly true in the dormitories. For a while it was my job to warm the bed of one of the big girls. I had seen other girls doing it and suddenly at the age of twelve or so it was made clear that it was my turn. At first that just meant wriggling up and down under the bedclothes to warm the cold clammy sheets whilst the big girl sat at the top of the bed reading. Later I was asked to touch the girl as well: she wanted her legs touched on the inside and her stomach caressed; she wanted to be stroked gently. She never asked me to touch her 'down there'. It was a gentle thing, an innocent thing; it obviously had its sexual connotations though I didn't realise it at the time – it was just the need for some kind of physical contact. So you had to touch and caress and if a nun or Miss Carberry came in, you had to lie completely still, buried under the bedclothes, and not move an inch. When the moment was right you got a kick and that meant it was all over, time to leave. To do this you had to crawl under the other beds without making a sound, and only when you'd checked that it was totally safe to do so did you get back into your own cold bed.

Sarah Louise decided to tell and informed the nuns that there were big girls who made the little ones do bad things to them at night and as a reward she got a severe beating. Sister Kevin was beside herself with rage and said Sarah Louise was the most 'disgusting and impure girl who had ever been at Moate'. She accused my sister of being possessed by the devil and again attacked about her roots. 'You're from the slums of Dublin! You should have left your dirt in Dublin!' Sister Kevin's stick rained down on my sister's body as she said it. She was flogged on her hands and her legs and straight across her back as we all looked on in horror. No one said a word and I'm ashamed to say that all I could think about as my sister was beaten within an inch of her life once again was my terrible anxiety about what the knock-on effect her dirty words would have on me. Needless to say that night the dormitory was even more subdued than normal. No one went into anyone else's bed and nor did they the following night. Sarah Louise was told to take her mattress out on to the landing and sleep alongside the statue of the Virgin Mary for the rest of the week – but 'even that was too good for her'. Sarah Louise was once again very ill after this flogging. Sister Aquin came to her rescue and temporarily stopped the beatings.

Each autumn we received a new list of chores and each year I prayed that mine would be working with Sister Aquin who was nice to us. I felt privileged working with her in the nuns' chapel (which she was in charge of) and somehow, with her, cleaning didn't feel like drudgery. For a while my job was to dust the chapel and polish the floor and I liked that a lot because it was a dry job; it was a wooden floor and didn't require being immersed in water or scrubbing. Then I went into the Sacristy to tidy up after the priest, and I did it really properly, putting it all back just so, exactly as Sister Aquin had shown me. I could have done that for ever, but unfortunately the jobs were all rotated and in time I moved on once again.

Mother Malachy was the manager of the school and her office was just off St Martha's where the cooker lived and the bread bins were stored. Her office housed all the records of the Industrial School and we were very frightened of what they contained, but we were even more scared of Mother Malachy. She was a horrible person and we all lived in dread of her. She was in charge of everything to do with the day-to-day running of the school.

I cleaned St Martha's for a while and was very aware of how close Mother Malachy was; her nearby presence was enough to make me feel highly nervous. I was always worried I would knock something off and break it, or bang down one of the lids too hard and she would come out of her office and be very angry with me. I was always on edge. I polished the huge locked bread bins so carefully. I wiped and polished the windows and the cooker till they shone. I got down on my hands and knees on the small quarry tiles which covered the floor and rubbed the polish on inch by inch. Then I stood up and polished the tiles so carefully with the dusters under my feet. I never once made the cloth like a scooter and did it on one leg. In time, I knew every inch of that floor, every nook, cranny and indentation and sometimes I could feel Mother Malachy's eyes boring in to me as I scrubbed away. If I caught her eye I would say in my best sucking-up voice, 'Is that all right, sister? Is that how you like it, sister?'

So I was outside Mother Malachy's room every day while she sat at her desk and rustled bits of paper. Sometimes she would throw a handful of raisins on to the floor outside the door of her office and they would scatter everywhere on the floor I'd just cleaned. I took this as a sign that I had pleased her with my careful, quiet cleaning and would scamper after them and eat them. I was always starving hungry, my belly rumbling by this point in the day and they were sweet and juicy. It could have been such a nice gesture but it wasn't. It was supposed to be a treat but it just felt humiliating. I could not understand why she didn't hand them to us. Why did we have to chase after them on the floor like field mice? One of the other girls said Mother Malachy got pleasure from seeing us scavenging on the floor like beggars; it reminded her of how important she was.

It was a sign that you were favoured if you got thrown the raisins and certainly they were a regular part of my cleaning near Mother Malachy's office. There was nothing else to show that she liked me, she was impassive and her heavy-set features rarely showed any emotion. One day though she came out of her office and stood in the doorway examining a piece of paper she had been studying and said, 'Your mother is more sinned against than sinning.' She didn't say it particularly kindly or gently, she just plucked it from the air and then made it clear that she had nothing more to add. I wanted to say something but I couldn't – we simply didn't speak back to the nuns. But any mention of my mother worried me because no one at Moate ever said anything good about Mammy. Yet I could tell from Mother Malachy's voice that it was not a cruel thing she had said – so what did it mean?

Afterwards I turned that piece of information over and over in my mind. She seemed to be saying that Mammy wasn't a sinner after all. She was *more sinned against* . . . Part of me wanted to tell my sisters, but since I wasn't exactly sure what it meant I kept it to myself like a little secret. It was the first time anyone at Moate had said anything vaguely nice about Mammy and I treasured the comment.

Chapter 13

Whenever Sister Bernadette had a cold or a cough she was always hacking up mucus into a handkerchief. And then she would choose someone in the classroom to do a horrible thing, and more often than not that person would be me. She would say, 'Kathleen, go into the nuns' toilet and wash my handkerchief out.' She would hand it to me and it would be quite revolting – slippery to the touch and cold. I had to wash the hankie, slimy with phlegm, out in cold water and hang it on the edge of the basin to dry. I was nine years old and in Third Class, which was taught by Sister Bernadette. This went on throughout the year and why she always picked me I didn't know but I thought it was probably because she had seen my records and knew that I had done dirty things.

Sister Bernadette was one of the more cruel and vindictive nuns. She took every opportunity to hurl psychological abuse at us. 'Those O'Malleys! What can you expect of them with a mother like theirs! A family of troublemakers!' It was never-ending – the constant chipping away at our sense of worth. But I still tried to be good at something. We were still being taught Gaelic by Sister

Cecilia. One day we were asked to write a whole composition in Gaelic and I was determined not to let it get the better of me. I knew I could do it easily in English so it shouldn't be too difficult in Gaelic. I started to feel really pleased and confident. It was about some birds and the nest they had made in a chimney. The words came very easily and although I wasn't sure I'd got all the past, present and future tenses perfectly correct, overall I decided I'd made a really good job of it. I sat there with my carefully prepared work. Sister Cecilia came sweeping down the aisle towards me saying in her booming voice, 'Now, Kathleen O'Malley, let me see what you've done.' Then she read my essay. I was so convinced this was a brilliant piece of work, I sat there patiently waiting for the praise I felt sure would be forthcoming. I did notice that her chest was heaving faster and faster and her colour was getting more and more ruddy, but I put it down to the wonderful work she was reading. Suddenly she said, 'Kathleen O'Malley, are you sitting for your Primary Cert?'

'Yes, sister.'

'Do you expect to pass?'

'Yes, sister.'

'Never mind, you wouldn't earn a farthing more if you had.'

I had no idea what she was talking about. She went on.

'I've never read anything like this before.'

'Thank you, sister,' I said, still blissfully ignorant of what was coming.

It wasn't until I heard her mutter, 'What can you expect?' under her breath that I realised she had been anything other than blown away by my Gaelic masterpiece. It took a moment to sink in that I had been crushed, utterly crushed, and as a horrible sense of self-pity started slowly to descend on me, she went over to one of the day girls and said, 'Now I'm sure you've got a better composition.' She read that girl's work and a big smile spread across her face. 'Now *you* could be a writer.'

*   *   *

I failed my Primary Certificate when I finally took it at the age of fourteen. I was desperately shocked and upset because I'd prayed and prayed to God to help me pass my exam and had worked hard. I knew I did not understand Gaelic very well but I used to have dreams of speaking it fluently and I was convinced this would have filtered down into my exam paper. When I told Sister Cecilia how distressed I was not to have passed it, she turned to me and simply said, in a very matter-of-fact voice, 'What do you expect? You're an *amadán*.'

By this time I was working on the hall door. School life had ended and full-time work had taken over. Certain girls, if they were showing any academic strength at this point, progressed up to the boarding school itself for further education. I was never considered a worthwhile pupil for secondary school, I was only suited for service like scrubbing floors and the like, but Sarah Louise had gone there at the same age, as Sister Acquin managed to get her in. But I was not considered to have any native intelligence at all and had to start working full time for my keep. It was decided that I should be moved on to the front hall at the convent, to open the door when visitors arrived and welcome them in, to collect and sort the post for the nuns and to run messages into the town when needed. This was considered quite an honour and a very special job – better than working in the orphans' kitchen or the laundry, and to me it was my first taste of freedom and responsibility in over six years and seemed positively heaven-sent.

One of my jobs was to prepare Father McKeon's breakfast. Every morning he had grapefruit sprinkled with sugar which I prepared two to three days in advance then put away in a cupboard to allow them a chance to marinate in their own juices. I was always so starving it was a major act of self-restraint for me just to sprinkle on the sugar and close the cupboard door. One day I gave in to temptation and spooned out the juice which had collected and drank it down. It was so delicious! It was like nectar. I gulped it down and even squeezed a few more drops out. When I realised what I had done I panicked. The grapefruit, which was due for the priest's breakfast that very morning, was no longer caramelized and moist-looking at all, so I hastily topped it up with water, sprinkled a little more sugar on top and prayed to God for a miracle. When Sister Agnes served it to him, I hovered around nervously finding an excuse to polish the doorway to see if he noticed anything. He took his first mouthful and ate that and then he ate the next piece and he didn't seem to have noticed anything different at all. His bowl came back with all the fruit eaten and not a word was said. I was so relieved I could have jumped for joy. But having done it once and got away with it, I got bold and did it again. I knew that one day it would be found out but my need was far greater than my fear and I didn't care.

My job on the hall door in Moate meant I could smell the odours coming up from the nuns' kitchen, and they literally made me go weak at the knees. The smell of meat cooking, potatoes roasting, fruit pies baking practically made me delirious and I would fantasise about being given a plateful of hot steaming food, but of course it never happened. Sister Chantelle was in charge of the nuns' kitchen and she was a very good cook; the standard of food that came out of it bore no relation whatsoever to what we were fed on a daily basis. A former orphan called Eileen Smith used to skivvy under her, and I tried to befriend her but she was really mean and wasn't having any of it. I would wait my opportunity if she was serving or something to try to steal some food but she had eyes like a hawk and used to guard the nuns' food as though it were gold. She used to pass the food through a serving hatch called the bend and the nuns took the plates from her the other side. Sometimes there was a split second when she had her back to me and I could grab a nice crispy roast potato, all sticky and caramelised from the meat juices.

I wasn't allowed to serve the nuns, but I was allowed to serve the farmers, Jimmy and Paddy Burns, and the two farm hands in the pantry where I prepared the grapefruits in the morning. Their food was pretty good too. I would serve them theirs then I would sit down with mean old Eileen to eat the leftovers. This pantry was a little dark room which had been a passageway. It had a small window and I used to sit there eating my leftovers watching the nuns passing by like penguins in a long line on their way to chapel. While we sat at this little table I remember asking God if he could do anything about my failure at Primary Cert and whilst he was about it *please* could he give me nice legs, not stumps of trees. That was all I wanted out of life and of course he didn't act on either count.

The first time I was asked to run out into the town on a Friday and collect the nuns' fish, which arrived by special delivery on the local bus, I just couldn't believe my luck. I had been locked up for so long, it seemed incredible to be allowed to make a trip out unsupervised. They also asked me to take one of the metal urns that were used to boil water for the evening cocoa along to the town garage because it was leaking and needed soldering. It was a big, awkward thing to carry but I wasn't complaining. Up until now I'd only ever been into Moate on a Sunday when the shops were closed up anyway and now I was being permitted to go in when they were open and run erands for the nuns. It was so exciting! I no longer had any desire to run away; it was simply the feeling of liberty which thrilled me.

I loved doing the nuns' shopping and after that first visit probably went out every other day. I would go to the shops with whatever order they had given me. After a while, one of the shopkeepers took a bit of a shine to me and he would detain me in the shop until all the other customers had left; it was almost a game that he set up. After a couple of visits he asked me to give him a kiss and I said I wouldn't do that and he said, 'Oh, it's only a little kiss and I'll give you thruppence.' Then he dropped the money on the floor. I bent down to pick it up and then scarpered before he could grab my arm. He tried it a few times and I would allow him to kiss my hand a bit because I was getting money to buy myself sweets. I never kissed him, but I pretended as if I might be going to and then I would run away. On one occasion though he very nearly succeeded in grabbing me, but someone came into the shop at that precise moment and he tried to cover it up by saying he'd been helping to put the groceries in the basket or some such excuse.

Like the rest of the girls in the school, I had no knowledge of sex or puberty or the outside world. This was the nearest I got to it – being groped by the horrible shopkeeper when I was out doing the messages. I didn't know any better. I had no way of knowing what the normal rules of behaviour actually were. I had no understanding of what he was trying to do but it worried me nonetheless; it was a warning. I didn't think it was the same as what Luke McCabe had done to me but it still made me feel anxious. I might have had my innocence taken away physically but I was still mentally unaware of sex and not adept in these awkward situations. But while I was very innocent in most respects, the one thing I did know was to keep my mouth shut because otherwise I would have privileges taken away. Eileen Smith had said to me one day, 'Everyone in the town thinks you orphans are eejits anyway.' It was a stinging remark and it hit home; I kept quiet because I knew no one would ever believe me above a respectable shopkeeper.

There was another man who laid his hands on me around this time and again I didn't report him because I knew there was no point. He was one of the manual workers from the farm whom I served at lunchtime and I never did know if he planned it or just seized an opportunity. I had to go downstairs to the furnace room one day and he was down there, in this little dungeon-like place, and he clearly saw me unsupervised, saw his chance and grabbed me and tried to kiss me. I was fourteen or fifteen by now and he was a young man in his early twenties. He was quite strong but somehow I managed to get out of his grasp and run away up the stairs. I think I was very lucky. I saw Sister Agnes when I got to the top a little out of breath but didn't say anything.

When I worked on the door, there was a young girl who came for piano lessons on a Saturday. Her father was a Church of Ireland vicar in the nearby town and they lived just down the road from the school. Although he was a different denomination he entrusted his daughter to the nuns to teach her music which they were well known for. I always remember her coming in and having her lesson and afterwards one of the nuns taking her off to the chapel to pray. And I was so indoctrinated by this stage I prayed for her too. After all she was a Protestant and so she was damned. I knew the nuns tried to convert her, to save her soul. They must have told her that this was 'their little secret' because thinking back she couldn't have gone home and told her daddy what went on after they'd finished playing the piano or her lessons would have been stopped.

Every day I put on my special black dress, short white apron and white headdress which was my maid's uniform and every day I saw Bridie put on her new clothes to go to the boarding school and although I liked my job, I did wish we could change places just once. Bridie had been at the school since she was two years old and she was a feisty, strong-willed girl and I envied her because they never did break her spirit. On one occasion though, following a public beating in the refectory from Sister Kevin for some minor misdemeanour, Bridie called Kevin a pig. She said it under her breath but Kevin heard, or thought she heard, so she asked Bridie to repeat it. 'What did you call me, Bridie Slevin?'

'Nothing, sister.'

'I heard you!'

'No, sister, you didn't, sister.'

'Yes I did. Right, girl, hand out and I'm going to slap you until you tell me what you said.'

Then Bridie did what we sometimes did when we were feeling particularly rebellious: she put her hand out then pulled it back at the last minute, and Sister Kevin hit herself. This enraged the nun so much she then gripped on to her tightly by the wrist and gave her a really loud whack on the hand with a ruler. Then she gave her another one. Eventually Bridie Slevin gave in and admitted she had called her a pig. 'Right, I'll show you who's a pig. When you go to school tomorrow, you will wear rags. You will not wear your uniform.'

And she saw it through. The following day Bridie was made to wear the smelliest dirtiest clothes, the ones that we used when we went to work in the far fields. She had to wear them up to the boarding school where no one had ever been seen in such rags. She stood out like a sore thumb. The nuns immediately knew that she had been up to no good and decided to punish her further. She was asked why she wasn't in her proper uniform. 'Sister Kevin's taken it from me, sister,' came the reply.

'Well, for that you will stay after school and clean the school.' So Bridie had to clean the classrooms after school which meant that she didn't get her homework done, which led to further punishment and so it continued, one thing after another.

My time in my new job was sadly very limited. One day I was just abruptly told not to go down to the hall door and to hand back my uniform. 'You won't be working there any more.' I was very upset and could not understand what had gone wrong. I waited for someone to tell me off and punish me but it never came. I was tortured by the thought that Father McKeon had complained that someone had been destroying his morning grapefruit of all its lovely flavour and that was why I had been dismissed. My imagination went into overdrive. Perhaps the priest had got very, very angry when he realised who was to blame. I worked myself up into quite a state imagining what might have happened and wondered if I ought to go to confession and tell all.

Perhaps there were others as well, but the main reason I was moved so abruptly was that my mother was due to make her annual visit that week and they couldn't have me opening the front door to her in my maid's uniform. I didn't know when she came, because we had no calendars or any way of telling what week or month it was, but as I later found out, my mother came on a specified day in the same week every summer when the school was relatively empty. They knew she never missed it. The last thing they would have wanted was me greeting her like a domestic servant because it would have been instantly clear that I was working for them, rather than being taught by them. What I also didn't know then was that my mother had been on their case anyway, asking awkward questions about our 'education' and they didn't want to give her any more ammunition.

I was unceremoniously removed from the nuns' hall and went to work in the orphans' kitchen. My job was to prepare the food, chop up the vegetables and wash the dishes. Sister Kevin would oversee and Sister Vincent occasionally came and helped out. It was a soulless place, no one took any pride in the food being cooked, only the amount. Sister Kevin meticulously counted out the slices of bread for their scrape of butter and there was never even one piece extra. Sister Kevin was very much in charge but she didn't like getting her hands dirty; we did all the work. When she did have to get involved with something dirty she would put on a blue and white fabric cuff which was elasticated at one end, to pull over her sleeve and protect her habit. She also had a sizable checked apron to tie round herself. Cleanliness was next to godliness, after all.

It seemed to me that the nuns had two very different voices:

one for when there were visitors from outside, or the priest was present or their fellow nuns were in earshot; the other was kept strictly for admonishing us. Though they came from all over Ireland, their voices when speaking to us bore little trace of their real accents and were uniformly hard and slightly flat-sounding. But there was one exception to that. Sister Aquin came from Kerry, she was the only nun with *one* voice – hers was a lovely, rounded, modulated voice: it sounded kind and it *was* kind. At one point when I was working in the kitchen every afternoon, I would hear her going up the stairs to her cell at around four and I would deliberately use bad grammar to get her attention and hear her speak – I loved the gentleness of her voice, which was like balm after the constant barrage of admonishment. I would say, 'What did you doing?' knowing full well it was incorrect and Sister Aquin would always fall for it and correct me.

'What *are* you doing, Kathleen,' she would say in her lovely sing-song voice.

The kitchen was below the level of the ground outside: all you could see were the nuns' and boarders' feet coming and going. When I worked there I used to look out of the small windows and see the nuns swishing by with their beautiful little polished shoes and neat black stockings. I daydreamed that I would become a nun too though I was never shown the slightest bit of encouragement in this direction. Lots of the nuns had come through the boarding school itself, but it was made very clear that I was not of the kind of raw material they were looking for.

It was during this time in the kitchen that I had my accident. I was working there permanently and no longer went out to the far fields each day. But when the others returned from their farm work and were looking forward to their usual treat of fruit tart for tea, I, in my new role as a kitchen worker, was sent off to take it out of the large double oven in St Martha's.

I bent down and heaved out the heavy dish containing a large rhubarb pie, big enough for seventy girls. I was a fairly small-boned girl and I struggled under the weight of the dish as I attempted to put it on the hot plate which was at shoulder height. As I did, my feet slipped on the rubber mat underneath me and the boiling hot juices from the pie spilt out and ran down on to my jaw, neck, shoulder and left arm. I felt a searing pain shoot right through me and screamed out loud. To my surprise Sister Kevin came rushing over and instead of looking as though she was going to kill me, had a very frightened look upon her face. I can still remember what I felt like, my skin burning from the hot juice, waiting to get a telling off from the nun for being so clumsy, and all she said, very gently, was: 'Go upstairs and get it dressed. – I will put ginger of violet on it.' I was really surprised at the change in her; perhaps it was the first indication I had of the seriousness of the accident and that maybe I hadn't been entirely at fault after all. Still crying I ran upstairs and she duly put an alarmingly purple dye on the whole area which just made it look worse but was apparently going to help it heal.

Not long after my accident, Mammy came in for her annual visit. Despite what was said about her, she wanted to believe that we were having a good education and a better life in the care of the nuns than she could have given us. She desperately wanted to believe that – you could see it in her eyes when she asked us how we were getting on. They had told her that Sarah Louise was carrying on her education when she turned fourteen and that had made her very proud. It was an indication that the nuns had brought out the best in her talented girls. And it gave credence to the lie she had been telling friends and neighbours for years and years that her girls really were away at boarding school for their education.

After I was burned, there was a very big scene. She couldn't believe what she was seeing. I was dyed where all the juices had spilt: there was a bright purple stain down my jaw, my neck, my shoulder and my arm. This purple dye didn't wash off – it apparently just wore off over time – and when she saw me it was still a vivid unnatural mauve. She took one look at me in the parlour and lost control. She rushed out of the door to the front hall where a whole gaggle of nuns was waiting. All her pent-up anger at how cruelly we were being treated came out. She screamed at the nuns, looking at Sister Bernadette in particular, 'Look at you! All you care about, you big fat lumps, is feeding your big fat bellies. Look at my children! They're starving; they're burned.'

There were so many nuns surrounding Mammy – they knew she was visiting and were expecting trouble, so had brought in other nuns as reinforcements – that I was scared for Mammy. I rushed in to take the blame for the accident myself. 'No, Mammy,' I said, 'it wasn't their fault, it was my fault. Please don't get cross.'

One of the nuns stepped forward and told Mammy to please be quiet, 'To remember where you are. This is a holy place of God.' But Mammy wouldn't shut up: she was absolutely livid. 'Please calm down, Mrs Byrne, you're an awful common woman. This is a convent! You must be respectful.' But Mammy carried on. She was getting more and more hysterical because she wasn't getting anywhere with them. She threatened to take us away with her. 'We're going to call the *gardai* if you don't behave yourself and stop shouting.' And in the end that's what they did; the police came and they had her thrown out.

We had been herded back to the orphanage by this point and so didn't see Mammy's humiliation at being thrown out on to the street. But we could hear the commotion and Mammy shouting and screaming as the policemen took hold of her and bundled her out. Inside I wanted to die. I had told her it wasn't the nuns' fault so why did she have to keep causing trouble? I could hardly look at my sisters but I just knew they were thinking the same thing: we would get no end of punishment for this. In the end Mammy's voice couldn't be heard any more but we heard the nuns talking to the police in the hallway and suddenly they were all nice voices and sympathy. What could they do with women like that? They were only doing their best but 'these people' were the lowest of the low.

We were never allowed to forget this incident. From this point forward the nuns had real ammunition to use against us. You could see the accusation in their eyes: your mother again, causing trouble. If we ever did anything wrong they came right out with it: 'What could you expect with a mother like that?' These accusations were so painful. I had never stopped loving Mammy but I'd spent so many years separated from her, I didn't know what to believe. By and large I trusted the nuns. We had to: we had no other authority figures in our lives and after many years of living in the institution we had become more and more institutionalised ourselves. We didn't have our own thoughts and opinions any more. We only had what they told us. In contrast we saw our mother only once a year and, like any children would, we wanted them to think well of her.

A few months later Sister Kevin overheard me saying something about Mammy to one of the girls and she decided that the message just wasn't getting through. She told me to follow her to the cloisters because she wanted a quiet word. She bent over to speak to me – she didn't want anyone else hearing this – and told me that Mammy was a bad woman. She caused more trouble than any of the other mothers put together. The reason why they thought so badly of her was because she walked the streets of Dublin. Did I know what that meant? I nodded meekly yes. I'd heard of it. I felt a horrible tight feeling inside my chest and she obviously saw that and decided she'd said enough. 'All right then,' she said, 'you can go.'

I went back to the yard, but I didn't want to play any more. I didn't want to see anyone. I went and sat on the bench and tried to work out how Mammy could be 'walking the streets of Dublin' and what that meant. Did that mean she was living rough like the tramps who used to sleep in our hallway? Was she homeless? Was she really 'in the gutter' now, another expression the nuns used to throw at us? I just didn't know what the words Sister Kevin had used meant, but I knew she wanted to hurt me. I turned it over in my mind again and again, but instead of dismissing it out of hand, I felt more and more strange and like I wanted to be sick but couldn't be.

Chapter 14

They had beaten us and, with very few exceptions, had crushed our spirits entirely, yet we couldn't hate them. Although they were figures of fear and torment they were also the Brides of Christ. They were closer to God than we were and it showed in every way. When they sang in the chapel it was heavenly, angelic. We always looked so scruffy and they always looked perfect. They wore a black habit, with the white starched front and rosary beads which stood out demurely over their breasts. Then they had a headpiece that went under the chin and revealed just the eyes, the nose and the mouth. No matter how much I hated them I desperately wanted their approval.

We watched their progress avidly. We were intrigued when we saw the new postulants arrive in their little bonnets with just a tiny veil; then after a period of time they became novices and wore a white veil and that showed they were on their way to being a Bride of Christ. Then, five years after they had entered the convent, they were professed and became a fully fledged nun. It was a very big day for the nuns, the priests and the bishop. I was once allowed to lay the table on one of these days and I felt excited just being in the room where the party was going to take place. It happened in the long dining room, adjacent to the priest's parlour where the priest had his grape-fruit. It had a long mahogany table and elegant chairs and lots of grand, ornate furniture and highly polished floors. I laid the table with the finest silverware and porcelain. I laid it out very carefully, just so. I was so happy to be in that room making it perfect for the nun's big day. I desperately hoped that someone would ask me to wait on the table and serve the food. I wanted to be part of it all: the nuns, the people, the excitement, the food, the party. But I wasn't allowed to; I was fifteen years old and I was simply allowed to prepare the room and then I had to vanish. I was tantalised by the thought that this was the last party the nun would experience in the outside world. This ceremony was, in effect, her wedding day and after this she would have the honour of wearing the full Sisters of Mercy habit.

I admired the postulants and novices because they were better than me and closer to God and they looked so pretty in their bonnets. More to the point I wanted to be one of them. There was this terrible adoration of the nuns amongst the girls: awe and fear all mixed together. They had been so spiteful, so cruel but I'd had it drilled into me that it was entirely for our own good and after so many years, I had ended up believing it. And they were a great mystery to us, mentally and physically. We were all obsessed by what the nuns had underneath their veil. Their headdresses were pinned so closely to their faces all you saw was a small circle of eyes, nose and mouth. We became convinced that they must be bald underneath it. That would explain why their headdresses were always fixed so firmly in place and never allowed to move. That would explain why they cropped our hair off when we arrived and kept it so short. Again, it was Sarah Louise who did what no one else dared to do. She caught hold of Sister

Kevin's headdress when we were sitting in the refectory having our tea, and attempted to pull it off. It was tightly pinned so she only got it a certain way, but we saw to our surprise that the nun did have some hair, which was quite a let-down really; we were a bit disappointed. I think we had thought the nuns were more like another species than they actually were. Sister Kevin was so shocked, she clearly thought my sister, whom she'd had so many battles with over the years, was violently attacking her and let out a piercing scream which brought several of the nuns rushing over to her assistance. Two of them held Sarah Louise down whilst Sister Kevin gave her a serious beating fuelled even more by the fact that my sister never did quite lose that slight smirk she had on her face.

They punished us but we believed and trusted in the nuns. They had to be right. We had been conditioned to think so. They were the Brides of Christ. They could only do good; they could do no harm. The nuns and priests were chosen by God to look after us. I never questioned that the beatings might be wrong, however unfair or spiteful they seemed. I knew that they were being meted out for our own good, our own salvation. And with no one else to talk to it was impossible to gain a different perspective. We were exposed to it constantly: we saw nothing else. We were in their care twenty-four hours a day, three hundred and sixty-five days a year. If the nuns slapped you, you must have deserved it. There was no way to avoid their chastisements. The only way I learnt to overcome the worst of their wrath was by buttering the nuns up and being sweet. 'Yes, sister, can I do this for you, sister?' I polished the floors obsessively to please them. I told tales on the naughty girls, the ones they wanted to pin something on, 'I saw Rita do it, sister, I saw her robbing it.' If it meant I could be in Sister Kevin's good books then I did it. I learnt from how the other orphans behaved and played the nuns' game.

* * *

One time Sarah Louise locked herself in the storeroom when my mother came in for her annual visit and just refused to come out. We had been given a whole shipload of bananas that year by a grey-haired gentleman who came to the school and presented them to us as a donation. We had been given a banana every day and they were slowly rotting in the storeroom. When my sister heard that my mother was in the school she locked herself up with all that fruit although it went totally against school regulations. Sister Kevin asked her to come out, but she didn't *make* her, which she would have done on any other occasion. Now I can see that she didn't insist she came out because it was their opportunity to get back at Mammy, to hurt her. I had to tell Mammy that Sarah Louise wasn't coming and she burst into tears and kept saying, 'Why?' again and again. The truth is I didn't know why either.

I didn't stop seeing my mother. I always wrote and went to see her when she visited, but I was starting to see her behaviour more and more as the nuns did. There had never been any proper communication when she came in and by the time I was fifteen I fervently prayed there wouldn't be. I didn't want her to get cross or blame the nuns for anything. We'd never had much to say to each other on these visits but now I stopped even asking about my brothers, or any part of her life. The past was not only dead, it had never existed. We stuck to safe topics and after a while in our letters and meetings just uttered the platitudes the nuns expected: *yes, we liked it there. Yes, we were working hard. No, we weren't any trouble.*

We knew that Mammy had been living in England for a few years by this time, though we knew almost nothing about it. Nor did we know anything of what went on behind the scenes but, as I found out afterwards, as Sarah Louise's sixteenth birthday approached my mother was told to apply to have her daughter returned to her. Although we all had to leave the Industrial School on the day of our sixteenth birthdays, the nuns often placed orphan girls in paid domestic situations if they did not have a home to go to. On the day that Sarah Louise had locked herself in the stores, the nuns had told Mammy in no uncertain terms that she would have to 'make a case for having her daughter returned to her' as her sixteenth birthday approached. Mammy knew better than to kick up a fuss about having to do this and humbly applied for my sister's release as she had comfortable lodgings and a job lined up for Sarah Louise at the Cumberland Hotel in Marble Arch, London where she also worked.

One day my big sister was at Moate and one day she wasn't. There was no ceremony and hardly any goodbyes. She just said that she'd write and would come and visit with Mammy in the summer. When my sister left, I didn't miss her, which would have been normal, I *feared* for her. I was very concerned that she had gone to England, to that Protestant land, to find work. Her soul would be in mortal danger! I pitied her, and made sure to mention her in my prayers over there in Satan's Land.

I'd had little or no contact with either of my sisters from the day we arrived. Sarah Louise's leaving was just a fact, I don't even think I felt jealous. I'd thrown myself into my spiritual life and had recently had quite a revelation about the Catholic Church. I remember the turning point for me came during one of Canon Pinkman's services at Mass during Easter. He had just finished his sermon and asked for donations. He emphasised that he wanted people to be generous, to put their money in an envelope and write their name on the front with the amount of money they had put inside. And he was up there in the pulpit and we were up there in the gallery and he called out the names of the parishioners and the amount of money they had given: 'Brendan O'Connor: sixpence; the Manning family: three shillings; the Murphy family: one shilling.' I remember hearing the names of some of the girls who were at the Primary School with me and realised that I was learning about people's respective positions in society. I remember thinking, Oh, they're rich, but they're not – they're only giving sixpence. It didn't matter that I was just a penniless waif – I had suddenly been given a glimpse of how the world worked. What mattered was that people saw what you did. It wasn't what was in your heart, it was how you displayed it. Of course I can see now that it demonstrates everything that's bad about the Catholic faith but as an impressionable young girl it was a very significant moment for me.

I did everything I could to please those nuns. I sang extra loudly in church, I worked my guts out in the kitchen and just prayed that one day someone would notice me. Since the day, after I had burned myself, that my mother visited and had to be thrown out, I had stopped mentioning her name at all. I knew they disapproved of my mother and in my final years at the school I started coming round to their way of thinking. I realise now what I didn't know then, that all three of us were slowly poisoned against her.

Failing my Primary Certificate had been like a body blow to me. It bothered me then and that failure stayed with me for most of my adult life. But I can't say I'm particularly surprised. We were taught not to think or question anything from a very tender age. The effect that had on me was to switch off all critical faculties and I became an automaton who wanted only to please people. And I was hardly ever at school. From the age of ten I was going to the laundry two full days a week, fifty-two weeks a year. I worked in the laundry and then the far fields, and the last couple of years I spent as the cook's skivvy, slaving away in the orphans' kitchen.

But I didn't feel angry as I came up to my leaving date. I had been brainwashed to think that the nuns had done the best they could by me. I was clearly thick just as they had said. I didn't feel angry that they had put me to work as a child because I believed that they always did what was right. I had become utterly institutionalised and had long since stopped comparing life at home to life in Moate.

I saved my anger and my dislike for the other girls. I felt little or nothing for them – they were *amadáns*, goms, eejits, tinkers; I had no time for their thieving or petty weakness. They were definitely further away from God than I was. With hardly any exceptions, except perhaps Maureen Slevin, I had made no friends in the entire eight years I had been at the school. I left Moate without the names of any of the girls to write to. We had spent eight years living together and failed to form a single relationship. We were still more like ghosts than children.

But the nuns! The nuns were another matter altogether. I felt so in awe of those women, my teachers and spiritual guides, and after everything I had been through, I just couldn't let them go. And the further I got away from Moate and eventually Ireland, the more I seemed to need them and their approval. I measured everything I did by what they would have thought of it. I could not break that bond – no matter how destructive it had been. I wrote letters and took presents and even my darling son to see them. I took embroidered handkerchiefs and perfumed soap and 4711 eau de toilette, all carefully wrapped in tissue paper. I did not care one jot for my fellow girls, but I so wanted those nuns to like me. It is a shocking thing for me now to realise how much I lapped it all up. They had kicked me and kicked me and kicked me and like a pathetic little dog I kept going back for more.

Chapter 15

My sixteenth birthday approached and preparations began for my leaving day. There was a specific sequence of events which all the girls went through as they got ready to leave, and although no one else was leaving on the exact same day as me, there were others getting ready to go soon after. In the months leading up to our departure we were allowed to make our going-away clothes or 'rig out' as it was known. It was so exciting working away in the new sewing room on these clothes to go home in. We produced two pairs of knickers which were made out of cotton with white lace round the edge and shaped like cami-knickers. We made a full-length slip and a home-made bra. Finally there was a grey dress which Sister Kevin helped cut out and then I made the rest. I'd been given a third- or fourth-hand herring-bone coat and a pair of new slip-on shoes. I really fancied myself in those shoes after the clumpy, workmanlike patched-up brogues I had spent the last eight years in. When I tried them on with the pair of nylons Mammy had sent me for Christmas, I remember the other girls saying, 'Oh you've got lovely legs, Kathleen. Oh, you've got lovely shoes, lovely stockings. You look gorgeous!'

On the day that I left I was awake very, very early. It was the day before my sixteenth birthday, the precise date that the government stopped paying for me to be there. I remember sitting on the edge of my bed pulling my nylons on so carefully because I didn't want to snag them with my rough skin and rough nails. In the end I got so nervous I would rip straight through them or ladder them I decided to put on the gloves that Mammy had sent me and do it that way. I put all the clothes I had made on and felt like a million dollars.

I was given a tiny brown cardboard suitcase to put my possessions in. Sister Kevin unlocked my cubicle for me and I carefully took out my beloved doll still in its original box, my fountain pen and pencil, my missal and my catechism and the little faded pile of letters I had received from Mammy over the years. They were my entire worldly possessions, everything I had amassed over eight long years and it fitted easily into the tiny suitcase.

I said goodbye to Lydia. I can remember the words to this day. 'Bye, bye, Lydia. I'll tell Mammy you were asking for her. I'll write to you.' I was so excited that it was finally my turn to be leaving, I didn't think of how emotionless and clichéd these words sounded; I didn't think for one minute of that poor little soul, left all on her own. I didn't think because in all the years we had been at the school we were like ships that passed in the night, there was no bond between us at all. The rest of my goodbyes were the same. I said it to everyone, but there was nothing excessive; no promises to keep in touch or come back to visit. I had spent eight years with these people but they were by and large the same sea of blank faces they had been on my first day at the school.

I left by the side gate as ever, not the main door. Winnie Carberry escorted me off the premises. She walked me out of the little gate at the bottom of the back yard. Then we turned left and next left and there we were in Station Road, passing the National School, and within minutes we were at the station. I waited on the platform and when the train pulled in, Winnie turned to me and said, 'Goodbye. Look after yourself. Don't forget to say your prayers.' The nuns had prepared me for my return to the wicked world. Their parting words had been: 'Don't forget to go to Mass and confession and to say your morning and night prayers.' They had given me some rosary beads, some medals of the Virgin Mary and St Christopher to wear round my neck and some novenas to say to the Virgin Mary, and some of the nuns asked me to keep in touch. I found this a bit strange, but stranger still was the feeling that it pleased me – it made me feel that I *did* matter to them.

Feeling very chic, very grown up, I sat on the train in my new clothes and watched the rolling hills of the country eventually give way to the chimneys and smog of Dublin. Three hours later I got off the train and Sarah Louise was there waiting for me, and we caught the bus together. I kept asking questions and not giving her a chance to get a word in. 'What's Mammy like? What's it like at home? What are the boys like? Are they lovely? Is Paddy nice?' I had only been on the bus couple of minutes but suddenly she turned to me with a look of pure exasperation on her face. She told me to stop shouting at the top of my voice and that I was an eejit, a culchie. 'Do you want everyone to know you've come from a school?' she said witheringly.

I remember walking towards the new house and feeling totally overjoyed, despite Sarah Louise's words. It was such a nice house and I just felt so happy to be going home there. Sarah Louise had told me that Mammy had married Paddy McNamara a year or so before and that she had gone to the wedding, and now there was a new baby! I walked through the front door into a nice lounge with a fireplace and all and there was Mammy at long last with Ian in her arms and he was having a bottle. I didn't want to but I felt immediately a little bit dampened. My fantasy homecoming hadn't quite been like this. In my dream version Mammy had rushed over and hugged me like she never wanted to let me go and there certainly hadn't been a baby involved. A terrible thought went through my mind: *I'm not her little girl any more.* As it was I didn't rush to kiss her. I sat on the edge of the armchair and said, 'Hello, Mammy.'

She looked up and smiled at me and simply said, 'Welcome home, Kathleen.' We both felt awkward and shy with each other. This visit was different – it was permanent and we were familiar strangers who would have to get to know each other again, and there was a lot to take in.

There was a pot of tea keeping warm on the stove and Mammy poured me a cup, still holding on to the baby. She gave it to me in a lovely china cup, unlike the enamel beaker I had spent so many years drinking out of. We didn't say much to each other, I just sat and enjoyed being home again.

Mammy had been given this new house whilst I'd been away. It was a corporation house, in a suburb of Dublin. When I went out for some fresh air later, I decided that it was a lovely spot. There were only about forty houses, all in a horseshoe shape with a big playing area for children in the middle. There was a Church of Ireland Primary School nearby and a rather genteel-looking nursing home surrounded by a large copse of trees: all in all it seemed like a delightful neighbourhood. But it was a small place and everywhere you looked people were standing out on their doorsteps chatting and passing the time of day. Mammy's words as I had left the house that very afternoon came vividly back to me. 'You must not tell people where you've been, Kathleen dear. If anyone asks you must say that you've been living with Granny in the country.' I didn't realise at the time how much stigma was attached to having your children taken away, how much shame Mammy had been living with for all those years, but I did understand that she was trying to make a new start in her new house and I would do what I could to keep the new slate clean too.

I shared a double bed with Sarah Louise and we had our own room. It was strange but nice to be in private again; to wash in the bathroom with the door shut; to go to the toilet unsupervised; not to have to sleep with thirty other girls all snoring or talking in their sleep. I didn't mind that I had gone back to a completely different situation from the one I had left. I'd never let myself imagine what home was going to be like. At first anyway I didn't mind that there were three new boys and a new stepfather, Paddy McNamara, to share our mother with, I was just so pleased to be back with Mammy. With hindsight I realise how strange that acceptance was. But I didn't question my emotions, I was almost entirely devoid of any feeling. I never thought about things. One effect of becoming completely institutionalised at Moate was that it never occurred to me to think about the relationships I had with people. I did not know what normal family relationships were like. I loved my mother and thought I did not blame her for what had happened. She never asked what had gone on at the Industrial School and I never tried to tell her. It was easier for us both to forget.

I caught sight of myself in Mammy's mirror the day after I got back. I had never been a skinny girl, but I hadn't really seen myself in a full-length mirror for years and I was horrified. I'd felt like a million dollars in my new home-made clothes, the first new things I'd had for so long, so I was quite surprised by this bulky-looking, pasty person who stared back at me. I'd had cheekbones when I went in and now where were they? My skin had a greyish pallor from the terrible diet we had been fed for so many years. And there was a bulkiness about my figure as a result of all that sugar I had consumed when I slurped up spoonfuls of the cocoa mixture. A combination of no fruit and vegetables, endless potatoes, fatty meat, and nothing of any nutritional value, had all taken their toll on me. I was horrified by what I saw in the mirror – I was completely without a waist; I had no shape at all.

Soon after my return, Mammy told me that she was taking me into Dublin to buy some new clothes. She was so considerate of my feelings; she never said that the clothes I had taken such trouble sewing screamed 'institution' and that I might as well have been carrying a large placard advertising the Industrial School I had spent the last eight years at. Without her saying anything unkind we went into Grafton Street and she got me to try on lots of different skirts and dresses. At first I kept picking up very large-sized clothes on the grounds that there would be 'room for growth' which was what we always did at Moate, but she just said very kindly and patiently, 'We'll get clothes to fit you now. Don't worry about growing into them.' She finally bought me several fashionable new outfits and I was as pleased as Punch. She put them on a slate because she couldn't afford to pay for them all at once. Each week a man came to the house and she repaid him in weekly instalments, then I took the payments over myself when I started work for my mother looking after the boys.

When I first went home, Mammy suggested that she pay me to clean the house, so that I'd have a little bit of money of my own, like my sister did with her job at the Cadbury's factory. She offered to pay me generously and I immediately said yes. Before leaving Moate my main concern had been how I would find work; I had assumed I would go into service looking after children, but I had worried, if I had to look after boys, how I would know what clothes to put on them or in what order!

And Mammy seemed very happy to have the majority of her family back under one roof with her again. She was very maternal towards all of us, constantly checking that we were well fed and happy enough. She kept an eagle eye on those little boys of hers, always making sure that they weren't being picked on when they played on the green in front of the house. She was quite prepared to fight their battles for them, intervening if one of the other parents got involved in one of their disputes, always the first to defend them.

She loved being a normal wife for the first time in her life. Every day her husband went out to work and when he came home Mammy would have his dinner ready. He had the lion's share of the food because he was the main breadwinner. Right from the start I didn't like that. It reminded me of how it was at Moate with the nuns' food compared to ours but I didn't say anything because it seemed to be what Mammy wanted. His slippers were there, ready for him by the fire. He would sit in his armchair after dinner, smoking his pipe, and Mammy would wait on him.

One night Sarah Louise told me in a whisper that, 'We weren't the only ones to have been sent away.' The reason Mammy was so protective of the two older boys was that they were taken off her too a few years after our own committal. I was so shocked by what she was saying, all I could think about was: poor, poor Mammy, she lost all of us. I had so many questions flying around in my head and stared at Sarah Louise open-mouthed in disbelief.

Sarah Louise went on. Because mammy wasn't married to Paddy McNamara, the two boys had been sent to an Industrial School when the littlest was only two and a half and it had broken our mother's heart completely. That, Sarah Louise said, was why she ended up in London. She'd never had the courage to tell us when she came in for her visits because she didn't want us to be upset. But when Sarah Louise and Mammy had returned from London to live in Dublin, they went to visit Paul and Bill at the school where they had been detained. They went there unannounced. Mammy said on the bus that she had a feeling things were not quite right. My sister said it was a horrible place and brought back a lot of memories she didn't really want to think about. Like me she had not talked to Mammy about what had gone on at Moate, she had buried those memories and was just relieved to be out. Since no one knew they were coming, they just walked in there and found the boys sitting in a room. They were scruffy-looking and uncared for and, worst of all, they were sitting in their own faeces. Mammy was terribly distressed but instead of bursting into tears, she just lifted Paul up in her arms and said, 'I'm taking him with me and I'll come back for Bill as soon as I've got more space.' She and Sarah Louise had been living in two fairly poky rooms and could only house one extra child. No one tried to stop her; they clearly did not have a leg to stand on. In response to her angry accusations that they had been severely mistreating her children, one of the nuns just said, 'Yes I agree. We're understaffed. We can't cope.' So they took Paul home with them and that night Mammy wrote a furious letter to the Education Department demanding to know what was going on. By the time she got the letter back authorising the release of both boys she had already taken matters into her own hands and removed Bill herself.

I was very shocked that this had happened to the boys as well but since Mammy never mentioned it herself, I kept quiet that I knew. I was determined to try to bury the past. I didn't want to rake over my mother's years of anguish and thereby add to it. I never told her about my lack of education and she never asked. But although she did not say much, her feelings about the Catholic Church had changed considerably.

After she got the boys' committal overturned she enrolled them in the local Catholic day school. But it didn't work out. Paul and Bill were both victimised and bullied and after a very short time, she took them out of there as well and put them into a Church of Ireland fee-paying school. Mammy just wasn't having it. She had finally got the majority of her flock back under one roof and there was no way she could bear to see any one of us being picked on. She had seen with her own eyes some of the horrors that had been inflicted on her flesh and blood and she could guess at a few of the rest. She'd had to deal with the boys' nightmares and bed-wetting when she finally got them home. I saw how protective she was of my step-brothers and I felt jealous of the attention she gave them. I wanted her all to myself as I always had done.

But Mammy kept a very watchful eye on me too; she was aware that the old rivalry with my sister was still there. She could see I desperately wanted to be like my beautiful older sister, and it just wasn't happening. I would try on her clothes, squeezing myself into her trousers, leaving the top button undone. Sarah Louise would find me and chase me round the house. 'I'm going to murder you; get out of my trousers, you big fat lump.' To escape I had to run up to our bedroom, imme-diately lock the door and stand the other side shaking like a leaf till she calmed down because otherwise I knew I would not have had a strand of hair left on my head. Anyone could see there was no great love between us.

One Saturday Sarah Louise said she and her friends from the factory were going on a bicycle ride and since I hadn't got a bike I couldn't come. Mammy just said, 'You can take the old bike, Kathleen will ride on your new one for safety.' And so that was how we set off, but once out of sight of the house, Sarah Louise demanded the good bike back and dared me to tell Mammy. I was nervous; I'd been locked up in an institu-tion for eight years and my control of that old bike was not good. I had no idea how you worked the brakes. On one of the country lanes with a car coming behind us, I started to feel wobbly and shouted at the girl in front to get out of my way but she didn't hear me and I ran straight into her. I grazed myself quite badly on my arms and face and Sarah Louise looked really worried. 'You won't tell Mammy, will you – she'll murder me. Tell her you were stealing apples and when the farmer caught you, you ran under some barbed wire and scratched yourself.'

We told Mammy that version. She didn't say anything until a month later when she sat Sarah Louise down and said, 'I know what happened. You made Kathleen ride the old bike. A car passed you and I know the man who was driving it. He told me everything.' Of course Mammy was making it all up but my sister didn't know that. She confessed all and was grounded for a month.

I tended to stay around the house a lot, helping Mammy and running errands. Goodness knows what my little brothers made of me. Not only was I a stranger, I was almost an adult. We had not grown up together and they were as unsure of our relationship as I was. They knew I helped Mammy and cleaned for her but they weren't sure if I had any real authority over them. One day when I had just finished cleaning the house, the two older ones came running in muddy and excited from a game of football with some local kids on the green outside. Paul, the eldest, just ran straight across the still wet lino floor in the hall in his filthy shoes. I was standing there with my bucket and mop and just saw red. I slapped him across the face and told him to get his dirty boots off immediately and not to kick the football inside. I did it before I had really thought it through, but it seemed to work because he duly took off his shoes, picked up his ball and sat down quietly in the lounge. Little did I know he was just awaiting the return of Mammy for all hell to break loose. He broke into heartrending sobs the minute she walked in the door.

'What's the matter with you, darling?' said Mammy.

'It's Kathleen – she hit me. She slapped my face.'

Mammy didn't need to hear any more. She turned to me and was very cross. 'Don't you ever raise a hand to my sons again!' It was the first time she had ever raised her voice to me. It hurt very much but I knew she was right. I was behaving as we had done at the school, not as we did in our house. At Moate, if a girl walked across a floor you were scrubbing you would lash out with a filthy cloth straight across her legs. But this was different. Mammy would never hit a child and I knew it. Her words struck me like a body blow. Somehow it made me feel even more as though *they* – the boys – were the family and I was the outsider.

Much as I loved being at home, after this incident I became determined to get myself a proper job, as I saw it, on my own merit, and I found a place working with a local family as nanny to their child and also their cleaner. Now that I had a regular wage coming in I gave half of it to Mammy for my board and lodging just as my elder sister did.

Once I was regularly contributing to the household, the way my stepfather was treated like the lord of the manor started to make me feel even more resentful than at first. I saw the money Mammy gave him if he went off to the pub for a drink or two; money he had given to her earlier on in the week ostensibly for 'housekeeping'. I started to add it all up and before too long it had begun to seem, in my selfish teenage head, that Sarah Louise and I were being rather exploited giving half our wages to this family who weren't really ours to begin with.

I applied for a job as a seamstress in Grafton Street. We had made our own clothes at the school and I thought I was good. I knew how to use a sewing machine with a pedal and could sew up and down seams perfectly confidently. They asked me to demonstrate my skills at the interview. For some reason the cloth seemed very unwieldy and I broke one needle after another. I didn't get the job, which just confirmed my concern about what I had learnt at the Industrial School. Did I have any skills fit for the real world?

After I had been working with the family for a while, I got a job at Jameson's, putting labels on the bottles of wine and spirits. A machine applied adhesive to the labels, then I would manually apply them. It was repetitive work but they hadn't asked for anything by way of references which was a godsend. My new job was also better paid than the nannying and meant that I could put a bit by each week. I was starting to feel as though I was getting somewhere in the world.

During that second summer after I left the Industrial School, Mammy surprised me by saying if we wanted to, we could come out with her to see Lydia on the Sunday. We hadn't been able to go back with her the previous year because she said it cost too much for all of us to go on the train, but this year she'd got a little saved. I jumped at the chance, not because I had so missed my little sister but because I wanted them to see the new me, the working girl, Kathleen. I wanted them to see how I had turned out.

The visit was a bit of an anti-climax. We were met by Sister Agnes at the hall door, and though the nuns seemed to smile more warmly than when we were actually there, nobody commented on the changes in me I felt had taken place since I had last seen them. Lydia looked pleased to see us, though she was as nervous as ever. She had been doing very well at the school and they were even talking about her staying on to take her university examinations. Sarah Louise and I asked about a couple of the girls who were still there and then she suddenly said in her slightly startled way, 'Have you heard what happened to Maureen Slevin?' We both indicated that no we hadn't and so, constantly checking the door to be sure one of the sisters wasn't about to walk in, she went on.

Two months after I had left, Maureen had also reached her sixteenth birthday but she wasn't allowed home because her grandparents had said they were unable to take her, or that was what she was told. She went into service to work for a doctor and his wife. But not very long afterwards she was seen back at Moate and the whisper got around that she was working in the kitchen. She had come back and made it clear to Sister

Kevin that she didn't want to go back to the people she had been placed with. Rumour had it that she'd been told to strip off her new clothes and put on a set of old rags once again. In front of everyone, Lydia included, Sister Kevin had shouted, 'If you won't go back to Dublin then you'll work in the kitchen.'

The next day they were heard fighting again. 'If you won't work with the doctor, you'll go to the Magdalene Laundries or Grange Gorman,' Sister Kevin shouted. This was the ultimate threat, the worst punishment – the infamous laundries or the local madhouse. Maureen was still refusing, so Sister Kevin started beating her and Maureen ended up curled up in a ball on the floor. Sister Kevin walloped her and walloped her and walloped her. 'You will go back, you will go back.' And that was the last time she was seen at the school and everyone said she'd gone back to the doctor after all.

I learned much later on, after I'd returned from Australia, that she's been so badly treated by the doctor and his wife that one day she just ran away. She went to the nearest beach and even though it was winter, she stripped off naked and walked into the freezing sea and drowned. She just couldn't stand her life any more, so she committed *suicide*.'

I felt shocked but I didn't feel any sympathy. I was more concerned for Maureen's soul which would be lost for ever – by taking her own life she had died in a state of mortal sin. I was quite worried about that. I didn't feel rage or despair or sadness because I did not know how to; not then and not later. Although I had known Maureen better than most of the other girls, her death didn't affect me. I just took it in a matter-of-fact way as we never had the chance to become true friends. It would take me years to feel anything more about her death than this numbness and to see what a tragic waste her suicide was.

We chatted a bit more but there was little to say. I looked at Lydia's dreadful haircut done by the nuns and felt a bit sorry for her, when I remembered that she was considered by the nuns to be someone with potential and I hadn't been, and those old feelings of worthlessness that I thought had been buried for ever began to come back. The best part of the visit was when we were leaving though the yard and everyone was staring at us in our nylons and heels and one of the bolder ones came up to me and said, 'You've got gorgeous clothes on, you have, haven't you!'

Soon after this visit, when we were back at home, lying in bed, Sarah Louise told me about a plan she'd formulated. The idea was that we would save up money from our respective jobs and when we had enough we would go over to live in London. It was a daring plan and I was just so happy to be included in my older sister's scheming, I went along with it.

Once a month Mammy insisted Sarah Louise take me with her when she went to a club out in Howth where her boyfriend played the bagpipes in a band. On my first evening out with her I wanted to wear my grey dress from Moate. I didn't see anything wrong with it and preferred to wear it even though Mammy had bought me new clothes. Sarah Louise took one look at me and said, 'I'm not going out with you in that culchie outfit. Hurry up and get it off or we'll miss the bus.'

At one of the dances I met a young man who also played the bagpipes and he asked me out a week later saying he would meet me in the village at the bus stop going into town. I was excited but nervous. I dressed up in my new clothes and Mammy walked me to the bus stop and told me to be home by ten p.m. I waited and waited but he never turned up and I went home feeling very let down. Mammy just told me that there were plenty more fish in the sea and added a word of warning, 'Kathleen, you'll have plenty of time. Just remember men will promise you the sun, moon and stars until they get what they want and then they will leave you.'

The next time I went back to the club with Sarah Louise he was there and started making his way towards me, but I turned away abruptly and that was the end of that.

Sarah Louise and I plotted our escape – as we saw it – every night. 'You'll just be a skivvy if you stay on here,' she said. 'You'll be paying to keep *his* children.' She had been to England, and although she hadn't seen much of it, she was sure the possibilities for progressing in life were far greater over there. She said it wasn't really like Satan's Land at all; there was nothing to be frightened of as we had always been taught. She knew she could do her nursing exams there which she couldn't have done in Ireland (because she didn't have a school Leaving Certificate) and she said that for me too it would be a good thing. We needed to spread our wings a bit. She painted a very convincing picture of how much better off we would be if we weren't giving away half our wages to a man we didn't really know. I had only been home a year and loved family life, but part of me desperately wanted to please my big sister and do whatever she said.

If Mammy saw the dissatisfaction on our faces she didn't let on. These were her good years and she didn't want anyone to spoil them. After years of waiting, she was married and respectable and had her own corporation house at last. The fire was lit every evening and there was always warm, nourishing food on the stove; life was exactly as she had dreamt it would be when she was growing up in Bohernabreena. But I could see that doors were not really opening for us in Ireland, that we would need to look elsewhere to spread our wings a bit. We told Mammy that we had applied for jobs at the Cumberland Hotel in London where she had worked and she went as white as a sheet and made it clear that we might as well have said we were off to the North Pole. She begged us, 'I've only just got you back, girls. I've got a lovely home for you here and you've got good jobs. Things will settle back to normal.' But we could hear the desperation in her voice and it made us even more determined.

I don't know when I started to feel resentful of Mammy but resentful of her I became. I know it was during the time I was at Jameson's; for some reason I got it into my head that she was at fault for having us sent away. In my immaturity I felt that if she had truly loved me she would have been able to protect me but she didn't. I saw her with Ian and the older boys, giving them the love I had longed for, waiting hand and foot on my stepfather, and I brooded on it and my bitterness grew. When she told me that she needed more money from me, from *my* wages, earned by *my* work, I felt quite put out. I did not want to pay for boys who were not my full brothers. I did not want to pay for a man who had the lion's pickings at the table. I chose not to remember the fact that all through our time at Moate she had inundated us with gifts and money which she had worked so hard to send us. I allowed myself to feel neglected and abused and the plan to escape gathered momentum.

Mammy could not believe that we were leaving again *of our own accord*. Deep down of course she knew that one day we would leave, she just hadn't thought it would be so soon. She pleaded with us, she got angry with us, she tried grounding us for a time, she said we had broken her heart. She did everything she could to keep us at home but in the end she failed. In secret Sarah Louise and I packed our cases and when she was occupied by the boys, we literally ran out of the house. I will never forget walking across the oval green and looking back and seeing her at the window crying and holding her head in her hands. Once again she had lost us and this time it was entirely our choice.

Chapter 16

I fled to England and if I had expected bright lights and endless opportunities, I couldn't have been more wrong. We saw nothing of London when we got there because we were working in a big, busy hotel: we had just swapped one institution for another. At the Cumberland we were housed and fed, only this time round the food was wonderful. But we wore a uniform and obeyed orders and it was immediately evident that as chambermaids we were amongst the lowest of the low. We were allowed a number of late passes per month depending on our age and status. In our position we were a great deal more restricted than the clerical staff and those with skills. But the work was not so arduous: ten rooms per chambermaid and that was your day done. And though I liked neither being addressed by my surname, nor the connotations of being a skivvy, and didn't feel very comfortable amongst the other maids, I liked the hotel and was reasonably contented with my lot.

Sarah Louise and I had met some RAF boys on the mailboat coming over and I started, tentatively, to keep in contact with one of them. The nicer of the two boys, Gregory, fancied my sister and I got the other one. When he tried to kiss me, his teeth had bit into my lip. I made it clear I wasn't very keen. He said he couldn't understand why I was rejecting him, I was lucky to have him interested in me. But I wasn't interested, so that was that. However, Sarah Louise was not interested in Gregory because she already had someone in Dublin, so she passed him over to me and I started writing to him. Various letters passed between us and slowly we became friends. Some months later we discovered that we would both be back in Ireland at the same time, so we arranged to meet up and in time we became boyfriend and girlfriend. He was stationed in Hereford and once a month we used to get together. Gregory was my first love, he was a lovely person, but even more importantly to me, he came from a very nice family. His sister was a nun, which was what I had always dreamt of becoming. And his mum was just what I wanted as well: she was stable and settled and respectable and in time she became like a surrogate mother to me. I didn't fully realise I had issues and hangups about my own mother until I met Gregory's. The longer I was away from home, the worse the problems with my mother became. I kept repeating in my head that scene towards the end of my time at Moate where she was shouting and screaming at the nuns and had to be thrown out of the school. I was afraid that a similar outburst might occur in my new life so I made sure she never got the chance. I wrote to my mother fairly regularly, but from that point on it had to be entirely on my own terms. I only ever took Gregory home once.

A short while into the job at the Cumberland, I saw a face across the canteen that I recognised from Moate. In later years, I reinvented myself so totally that actually meeting someone who had been to the same school as me would have been a total horror. But now, age seventeen, newly arrived off the mailboat and a bit green round the gills, I was happy to just see a familiar face. She remembered me as well and we chatted a bit and gradually got to know each other. She shared with a large jolly Irish woman and we used to spend a bit of time hanging out in each other's room. One day when I was in there, I noticed that draped on the bed was a Playtex girdle, a new type of corset that I had seen in the magazines and desperately wanted. I still saw myself as a big fat lump and was very keen on anything that promised to give me the figure I longed for. The one that Mammy had bought me was stiff and boned, but this one could not have been more different: it was made of soft, flexible rubber with perforations so that you could sweat and stay comfortable. Suddenly I was back at Moate and decided to 'borrow' it just as we had as young girls. We had a special term at school for taking something off someone else – *I'll mind it for you* – and that was what I did, I minded it.

I didn't have any intention of keeping the corset but that wasn't how the security officer saw it. My school mate had called her as soon as she realised it was missing and told the lady I was the only other person in her room that day. I was questioned. I was all innocence: *I haven't got it, honest to God, I haven't touched it.* The security officer looked in my drawers and sure enough it wasn't there. Then she suddenly turned to me and said, 'Can I have a look at what you're wearing underneath?' Still protesting my innocence I lifted up my skirt and there it was! I had completely forgotten I had put it on and so I was caught red-handed. She was very nice to me. She just said, 'Wash it and give it back and no more will be said about it.' That was very good of her. I had slipped very quickly back into my old ways and it could so easily have been very bad for me. But it was a good lesson: I didn't need to be told twice.

Sarah Louise had moved on to take up her nursing by this time. She had only intended the Cumberland to be a stop-gap and once she had passed her entrance exams, as she always knew she would, she moved out to Braintree in Essex. When she had applied, I had proudly told her of my plan to sit the exams the following year but she had turned to me with one of her most scathing looks and said, 'You! You're too thick. You're stupid. You're a gom. You'll never pass the entrance exam.' I was deeply wounded but privately decided she was probably right and didn't even apply.

I didn't get out of the Cumberland much; our days largely revolved around our shifts, but gradually I started making forays out from Marble Arch down Oxford Street to Regent Street. I loved looking in the shop windows at the new fashion. It was the end of the fifties and the shops were full of nipped-in skirts with acres of petticoats underneath and high heels. Sarah Louise had always been fashionable and within a year of being in London I was starting to follow the trends and be aware of what suited me. Mammy had got me interested again that afternoon when she took me shopping in Dublin and now I was able to go shopping with my own wages. The first thing I bought was a blue felt skirt with beautiful heart shapes stitched around the hem and a blouse to match. I liked myself so much in that outfit, I went and had a professional portrait taken. I had worn other people's clothes for eight years and now it was my turn to feel special. We were paid weekly, a certain amount was deducted for board and lodging and then we were free to do as we wished. I became quite a regular at Richard Shops, always watching the new styles as they came in. I developed a system and I was always very careful; I had best clothes and working clothes. I allowed myself a new outfit in the spring and a new outfit in the autumn and I sent money home to help Mammy out.

Within a few months of working at the Cumberland, I decided I wanted to move on to the clerical side. I spoke to Mrs Hancock, the head of housekeeping, who seemed to have a bit of a soft spot for me, and she spoke to the general manager and I got myself transferred to the letter desk. Along with the increase in status my wages went up quite significantly and I opened my first cheque account at Barclays Bank in Great Cumberland Place. I was always careful with my money and that day I deposited about one hundred pounds which I had saved since I arrived.

My job was to sort the post into the various pigeon holes and answer the phone on the enquiry desk. Early on I had a call from a man with an American accent asking were there any suites in the hotel. I had no knowledge of hotel vocabulary or the various rooms and their descriptions and simply said, 'No sir, but there are sweets in the Corner House.' Lyons had an establishment on the corner of the hotel and this sold nice confectionery, chocolates, cakes and teas: it was all I could think he meant. I put the phone down and thought no more of it. Fortunately no one overheard my error and I soon settled into my new post and started to enjoy it.

In one of her letters Mammy mentioned that a girl called Mary had called. She had been at Moate with us. On my next trip home I visited Moate and Sister Aquin asked me if I could get Mary a job. I wrote to her and said there was a job in the bookkeeper's office at the Cumberland. She applied and came over to England. She had always been intelligent and was quick to pick up the work. We shared a room in the annexe of the hotel overlooking the penthouse of Larry Parnes in Seymour Place. He managed a lot of the big pop stars like Billy Fury at the time and there were always interesting-looking people coming and going from his flat. Mary and I used to flirt with all these good-looking young boys; we would meet them down in the street and sometimes go back up with them to the penthouse when Larry was away, just to listen to music. It was all harmless fun.

During the time I was at the hotel I saw a poster advertising a talent show they were having at the Hammersmith Palais. Joe Loss, a very famous bandleader, was to be at the audition. I was so excited. I had always loved singing: at Moate it had been an escape from the daily drudgery. When the nuns sang I almost felt I was floating. I used to sing in the bathroom or bedroom at the Cumberland just to entertain my flatmates or my friends from the book-keeper's office. I'd even found myself a singing teacher who promised to send me to auditions but never did. Looking back now, she knew something I didn't! Still I knew that my day would come. I was quite convinced I was going to be the next Connie Francis and since I deluded myself I looked a lot like Brigitte Bardot, I felt quite sure it would prove a winning combination. I practised and practised the Elvis Presley song I planned to sing and was very confident that I was going to make a lasting impression. Well, I certainly did that!

I set out for the show with a whole crowd from the book-keeper's office. We were in high old spirits, having a lovely evening, but when my turn came and the music started up, my mind just went completely blank. I'd forgotten the words and Joe Loss had to prompt me again and again. With each prompt, my singing got louder and better, or so I thought until after I'd finished and was walking across the dance floor back to my seat and someone said, 'Are you a comedienne?' This comment obviously wasn't enough to thwart my ambition and I set my sights at another audition.

This time it was at the Granada Cinema on the Edgware Road. I chose a Connie Francis song. I still believed that I had talent, so was staggered to find I wasn't one of the chosen ones. Years later my friends who were in the audience told me that the sound had been turned right off in the middle of my number, but they hadn't had the heart to tell me. It makes me cry with laughter now at how self-deluded I was. I recognise myself in those poor creatures who enter *Pop Idol* with the same self-belief and an grateful that I came up before Joe Loss and not one of the judges on that show. Probably the only prompt I would have been given was – please leave the stage!

Whilst I was living in Australia Lydia finally left Moate and in due course followed Sarah Louise's path and studied as a nurse at Braintree. Once again Mammy did everything she could to keep her remaining daughter at home because, as my brother told me only recently, it had broken her heart in two that night when we had run away. She had by this stage come to view our supposed education as a curse for all it had done was to estrange her daughters and make them leave her. But Lydia was young and clever and, like us, felt there was nothing going for her in Ireland.

It was 1961 when I left for Australia. I had found out that it was offering cheap immigration visas for suitable applicants, I decided to give it a try. It was known as the ten-pound scheme and when I saw the advert asking for people who could offer something to Australia, I just thought, Yes, that's me. I was doing book-keeping by this stage and that seemed like a definite skill. I told Mammy what I was intending to do and she threw her hands up in horror and said, 'Over my dead body.' I needed her signature for the application form but she refused and so there was nothing I could do but forge it. It was only a little white lie, I told myself.

For the princely sum of ten English pounds I flew to Australia. It took thirty-six hours. I flew out to Melbourne with my savings from the Cumberland and checked into the camp for immigrants, which was horrible and crowded and I resolved to get out of it quickly as I had got in. I was lucky in the first few weeks because I got an introduction to a hire-purchase company who agreed to take me on as a ledger-keeper. On a typing course at night school I met a very friendly Scottish girl who was in the army and looking for a third person to share with her and a friend in a rented house she had found. I jumped at the chance and moved into a very pleasant house with them. Life was going well. For the first few months, my faith in God remained steadfast and unshakeable. I continued to attend Mass every Sunday, to go to confession and to pray fervently daily. I felt privately shocked that the girls I was sharing a house with sometimes had their boyfriends over to sleep at night, so I prayed for them too; I was determined to lead a sin-free and blameless life.

I loved my life in Australia but it was while I was living in Melbourne that I gradually began to lose my faith. There was no single incident that destroyed my belief in God. I just started to look around me and see that there were other ways of living. I came to realise that people who did not follow the strict Catholic teachings were nonetheless good and kind and, in many ways, less judgemental of others than many of my fellow Catholics. I went to Mass one Good Friday and came away totally depressed by what seemed to me the narrow-minded bigotry of the Irish priest who gave the sermon. Slowly, almost imperceptibly, I lost my belief in everything the Church stood for.

After a year in Melbourne, I moved to Sydney with a girl-friend from the office and got a job as a demonstrator for a company called Gala. I had two weeks' training where I was shown how to demonstrate the washing machines and how to cook various types of packet convenience food which I would also be selling. I didn't like it very much but I decided that needs must. And then I met Alan, the first man with whom I fell totally in love. He was a wonderful person and one night without really intending to – maybe we'd had a few drinks or something and were kissing and cuddling – we made love. I wish I could say it was marvellous and the earth moved but it didn't. I was nervous and it was over before it started. A feeling of intense sadness came over me and close behind a familiar feeling of being dirty and used. But for once these negative thoughts didn't last. Alan was very sweet to me, he was very easy immediately afterwards and I suddenly thought, That was nice, now I've become like the girls I'm living with. I felt like a normal woman at long last.

I had never had a relationship before where I was prepared to risk everything. But a year into our affair I discovered that I was pregnant. I never wanted babies. I knew how tough it had been for my mother and I did not want to struggle in the same way, nor did I want a child to suffer as much as I had. Although I was very much in love with the baby's father, and planned to marry him eventually, I just did not want events in Mammy's life repeating themselves in mine. The doctor I went to see tried to suggest adoption but again because of my circumstances that was out of the question. I went ahead with the termination and was overcome with terrible grief immediately afterwards. I was in a very disturbed state crying and asking for my mother and I remember the nurses telling me to be quiet. Alan arrived with a big bouquet of flowers and tried to comfort me but I was too wrapped up in my own pain. The abortion made me re-evaluate all the very hard decisions my mother must have made when she found herself pregnant with us. It made me question why I was on the opposite side of the world so far away from her and my old life. I had been running so fast I thought I had got away, but instead I had hit a brick wall. I knew I needed to return home to Dublin and see Mammy.

The company I worked for in Sydney managed to arrange an inter-company transfer and I was able to walk straight into a job on my return to Ireland. The only difference was that in Ireland Gala was called Hotpoint. I put the termination behind me as quickly as I could and got on with my old life. It was great to be back with Mammy again. Having fended for myself for a few years, it was wonderful suddenly to be part of a family again, kids coming and going, neighbours dropping by, a pot of tea always keeping warm on the stove. I met up with Gregory and his family and they welcomed me back into their midst. Everything was the same.

Chapter 17

Late in 1963 I had come back to be reunited with my mother, fully intending really to talk to her at last. Yet it still didn't seem to be the right time. I loved being near Mammy but I would only have it on my terms. I was very cagey about my actual work *address* because I was still worried that she might just turn up and create a scene as she used to at Moate. It didn't occur to me that she was not that sort of person: it had just been hardwired into me by the nuns that my mother was prone to outbursts and her 'visits' were to be avoided at all costs. I had worked hard for my job at Gala, I had been diligent and punctual and successful at selling; I could not risk my mother coming in, shouting and screaming and causing an embarrassment.

Having been to the other side of the world and back, now I could really begin to reinvent myself: having travelled gave me room for some mystery in my past. So I started to make myself up. I was out on the road demonstrating, moving from place to place and I liked the freedom of it. I was delighted to discover that the other demonstrator employed by the company was a boarding-school girl who had studied domestic science and got all her exams. And there we both were doing the same job! She was everything I had aspired to be at Moate and suddenly the playing field was level. I hadn't thought much of demonstrating washing machines when I had been in Australia, I had just seen it as a means of survival, but in Ireland, it had a certain status attached to it and I liked the company I was keeping.

I also started to get to know the director's personal assistant, Rita. She was a bubbly, well-connected, outgoing person who offered the hand of friendship as soon as I joined. Initially I was cautious – what if she found out what had happened to me? Sister Cecilia's words repeated loudly in my head: *Don't tell anyone where you were brought up because they will only look down on you.* But one day when Rita and I were chatting she told me she'd been to a Church of Ireland school and suddenly I knew I was safe. A different denomination meant that no one would be asking questions. She introduced me into her nice middle-class circles in Dublin and to a gentleman farmer called Dougie whom I started dating. I was still living at home, but socially I had moved into a world I had always aspired to: a world of hunt balls and dances, a world as far apart from my own as it was possible to get.

Dougie and I quickly became a couple. He was older than me by some fourteen or so years, but that term 'gentleman farmer' meant everything. Despite the fact that we were an item I kept my two lives firmly apart and never let my boyfriend near our house or my mother – he just dropped me in a country road round the corner and I would dash home.

I had visited Moate on my return and been received surprisingly warmly. I went on my own and was very nervous as I approached the main door. It had been like a prison to me for eight years, but suddenly I was welcomed in as though I were visiting old friends. Suddenly I had freedom to go wherever I wanted. I had roamed the beautiful, spacious grounds of the boarding school, the manicured lawns and rose beds, and sat by the summerhouse. I took a beautiful photo of the convent showing the boarding school and its lush gardens. On the back I have written 'school grounds' in neat handwriting. And yet you can't see the Industrial School, the laundry and the yard which was our domain; you can't see any part of the school I really attended. But I wanted my smart new friends to believe that I had grown up there and not in the orphanage. With that picture I was getting confirmation of my story; securing it.

It all came to an abrupt end some months down the line. A new girl on the switchboard started enquiring where I lived. She was a chirpy little thing and just trying to be friendly but immediately my mind started working overtime. When I told her my address, she said, 'I know someone in Raheny. What a coincidence! I've got a cousin who lives there.' To me this was far too close for comfort. I was in imminent danger of being discovered. I panicked and decided it was time to move on again. I had recently seen an advertisement for a job as an English-speaking governess to a family who lived in Paris and I decided to apply.

I filled in the necessary information on the job application and was surprised how quickly the lies had started to feel like the truth: boarding school, Leaving Certificate, stints in Australia and Dublin as a washing-machine demonstrator. They didn't mind that I couldn't speak a word of French – it was good enough for them. They said they had three children, two girls and a boy, they holidayed for a month in Venice in the summer and skied in Davos in the winter. They offered me the job by return post. They would pick me up from the airport.

It was all frightfully grand. The wife was connected to one of the more minor royal families of Europe; he too was an aristocrat. They lived in a beautiful apartment on three floors in the embassy area. I was to speak English to the children and take them to school in the Avenue Foch. I was to be treated as one of the family. We would all – Madame and Monsieur, the three children and myself – have lunch together in the salle à manger. There was a butler, a maid and a cook so I would not have to lift a finger in domestic duties. Our food, which was carefully selected and prepared, was sent up in the dumb waiter. If the children were having so much as an apple, it arrived peeled, cored and sliced.

Madame was never seen before ten o'clock in the morning. The children had to be prepared for school quietly without disturbing her; this was even true on the weekends. She break-fasted in her room then she sat in a chair in the exquisitely decorated salon doing a tapestry or playing solitaire until we arrived back from school. Apart from this she did nothing – she had no hobbies or interests. Sometimes she asked me to tell her about Australia just to pass the time. It seemed a strange life to me but she did not seem unhappy with it. Monsieur was also interested in my previous life. When he heard that I had spent a lot of time living in hotels he was very curious. I had more or less lost any accent, prided myself on my good table manners and knew I was fairly good at passing off by this stage. I was rather proud of the fact that you now couldn't tell where I came from.

In summer we duly went for a month to Venice as promised at my initial interview. We stayed in one of the royal palaces and it was a great eye-opener: if I thought there were a lot of staff at home in France, here there were three butlers and more maids than I could possibly count. It was very hot and sticky when we got there and before lunch I got the children changed into fresh clothes and decided to change myself. I put my worn clothes on a chair and came down to the dining room. When I came back upstairs, I found that my clothes were all gone and I just thought to myself: Thieving bloody Italians! They've nicked my dirty clothes! I didn't have long to dwell on the matter because we were due off to the Lido to swim as we would do every day on our vacation. It was just as well I had kept my thoughts to myself for when I got back, my clothes had been returned by the maid washed, pressed and hung up in my wardrobe. We lived in great splendour: I even had my own personal maid to help with the children when we took our daily trip on the ferry to the Lido where they had their own designated little cabana at the Excelsior Hotel. The sun shone, I loved Venice, and Coosan Point and Dollymount, the beaches of my own childhood, seemed like a dim and distant memory. I'd gone from one extreme to another – absolute poverty to a life of absolute indulgence.

Back in Paris again, it hit me afresh how dull their life really was. They had everything they could wish for but you never saw any warmth or affection or shouts of laughter or play-fighting. They modelled themselves on the royal family of England and the children were impeccably brought up, but they never saw anyone else. The school they attended had two children to a class. They did not have friends round after school or go to friends' houses to play. I became very fond of the children but the more I watched them and their life of great privilege, the more dismayed I became. Neither their mother nor their father seemed to pay any real attention to them. When their grandmother came over from Greece, the older girl always said she had been constipated which brought on a good deal of fuss not to mention soap and hot-water bottles and the like. I knew she was all right, she just craved attention.

It was a good life and I wanted for nothing. Neither did the children except, it seemed to me, the love of their parents. So really their childhood was in a way as deprived as mine had been.

In the end, after nine months, I decided I wanted to go home, and I handed in my notice. Soon after I returned I got back in touch with my old friends at the Cumberland and the Duty Manager asked me if I'd like to become a housekeeper. The position came with a room which I wouldn't have to share with anyone else and a bathroom ensuite. I jumped at the chance. But this promotion was double-edged. I was always watching my back. I was convinced that everyone knew that I had once been a chambermaid and that they looked down on me because of it. I was cagey and defensive and the chip on my shoulder grew larger by the day.

Some months passed. One evening a friend made a casual remark that would change my life quite considerably. She mentioned that a friend of hers worked in the beauty business and why didn't I consider it? At first I was very dismissive. I hardly even wore make-up, just a bit of lipstick, and felt that anything else was strictly for street girls. Her suggestion clearly sowed a seed, though, for a couple of days later I gave Elizabeth Arden a call and asked them to send me an application form. Two weeks later when it still hadn't arrived I phoned them up and curtly asked them if they thought that was any way to run a business. The secretary on the other end was highly apologetic and arranged an interview for me then and there.

The interview went well and I got the job as a beauty consultant in their Old Bond Street premises. After a two-week training period I was allowed on to the floor of their very elegant salon, complete with sumptuous hand-painted Chinese wallpaper and crystal chandeliers. My job was to sell cosmetics and beauty products to the ladies after they had received their facials, massages, pedicures and waxings. The treatment girls would have written down the preparations they had recommended and it would be my job to sell as many pots and jars, lotions and creams to them as I could. The salon was one of the first of its kind in London, had an excellent reputation and was a very refined atmosphere to work in. The ladies were all feeling fairly pampered by the time they got to me and I found it easy to sell to them. Some months into the job I found myself selling to this young Indian girl who had come in with her father and was buying every cream I recommended. Having chosen quite a selection she then said she liked the eye make-up I was wearing and could I show her that as well. I had to think fast. I wasn't wearing Elizabeth Arden, because I couldn't afford it. We only got a ten per cent discount and on our wages it simply wasn't viable. Anyway I pulled out a few colours and showed her how I had 'mixed it'. She was quite happy with that and added those to her list as well. Tracey, the deputy manageress, saw it all going on and once the girl's father had paid for everything came over to me and said, 'That was a very good sale.' But before I could start basking in a little glory, she took me aback by saying, 'But you're not using Elizabeth Arden, are you, Miss O'Malley?'

'No' I said, 'I can't afford it. I'm still using Max Factor at present.'

'Oh, I thought you would be using Gala?'

'But why should I use Gala?'

'You worked for them.'

'Oh!' I said. 'I worked for Gala in Australia; they had the Hotpoint dealership out there. I was demonstrating washing machines! Did you think I'd worked for Gala, the make-up people . . . ?' My voice tailed off as I realised that not only Tracey but probably the rest of the people who had interviewed me had assumed the companies were one and the same. For once this hadn't been an intention to deceive on my part, I had never assumed anyone would make that connection. I had just given the dates of my employment in Australia and Ireland and clearly they had believed I was a very experienced make-up consultant.

Fortunately I didn't lose the job when they realised that they had hired me on a false premise, they saw the humour in their mistake. I stayed on and actually started to progress within the company. I always had a chip on my shoulder about people who spoke nicely or who seemed overly refined, but I gradually came to understand that this was something I was going to have to get over. Elizabeth Arden had the Royal Warrant and really took itself very seriously. Princess Margaret visited the salon on a regular basis and there was a designated treatment girl who would treat the Queen Mother at Clarence House. We had royalty visiting us, politicians, film stars, international socialites. Mrs Irving the buyer fluffed around importantly, gossiping about one client, sucking up to another. And although I found quite a number of the staff stuck-up and somewhat condescending, overall the work appealed to me and I decided to apply for the training course at Grosvenor Street to become initiated into the arts of the treatment girl. Despite the fact that this was going to cost me one hundred pounds, I was determined to do it because I so desperately longed for a qualification.

The treatment girl had status. She had her own room and clients were brought to her from reception. She had one client an hour every hour. In between a maid would pop into the room, tidying it, warming the wax, getting the room ready; she did not have to lift a finger to prepare or clean the room herself. I was hungry to get on. Having repeatedly failed my school exams and been considered too unintelligent to become a nurse, I jumped at the chance to get a professional qualification. I was learning a skill, moving on. I would have something else to offer. Another door would open for me.

By this stage I had a boyfriend called Giorgio. He lived in Rome. He had been over watching the Italians play football and I had been introduced to him by an old friend. We hadn't spent very much time together, but it was getting quite serious and knowing that Elizabeth Arden had a salon in Rome I applied for an inter-company transfer. When I spoke to the personnel officer about it she appeared to be sympathetic but just said there were no vacancies in Italy, but there was an opening in Wellington, New Zealand. Having floated the idea that I'd be keen to move I started to feel worried. What if they thought I wanted to leave? It was well known that for every girl in the Old Bond Street salon there were ten girls out on the road in the UK waiting to take our jobs. Though I didn't want to go to the back of beyond (I had been to Australia and that was far enough) I didn't want to be in a position where I was beholden to them. I attended an interview in Grosvenor Street and at the end asked about the salary. She explained that it was a three-year contract, the company would pay my airfare there and back, and I would get thirty N.Z. dollars a week. I didn't have a clue what the exchange rate was but that sounded quite a healthy figure compared to the fifteen pounds a week I was getting in London and I said yes.

I decided to go and see Giorgio for a few days before I took up the post. Elizabeth Arden arranged all the flights, including a stop-off in Rome. I was aware that this might well be our goodbye. Giorgio was something of a good-time guy, hardly a letter writer, and the relationship was unlikely to stand the strain of a three-year separation. But there he was waiting for me at the airport, as handsome as ever. Any lingering sadness was dispelled when he whisked me off in his sports car and we had a wonderful time driving round the city stopping off at cafés and art galleries and bars. He spoiled me rotten and called me his Irish rose. Whilst I was there Elizabeth Arden had arranged for me to get my hair done in their salon as a complimentary treatment. It was a lovely treat and I was just relaxing into it, chatting to the hairstylist about why I had accepted a transfer to the other side of the world when she told me they had a vacancy in Rome. I couldn't believe my ears. I was absolutely dismayed but what could I do? All my ongoing flights had been arranged. They had taken press pictures of me, highly made up, for the launch. I knew there was no way out.

Giorgio suggested that I extend my stay a little longer before going to New Zealand and I thought why not. I had always had decisions made for me and for once I was going to be rebellious and do what I wanted. He offered to notify London, Hong Kong, Sydney and New Zealand of my delay, and I was happy to let him do so. Those extra days were the most exciting time in my life up to that point. It was thrilling to have stepped off the straight line I had always walked. However, I knew it couldn't last. I had to honour the three-year contract I had agreed to. The day came for me to leave and parting from Giorgio was painful. I left Rome in 1970 tired and not knowing what the future held for me, but with no regrets, as for the first time in my life I had been carefree and enjoyed it.

Once in New Zealand I quickly worked out that my thirty dollars' basic wage was not worth what I had calculated. Even worse, the tips which had made up a hefty proportion of my salary in Old Bond Street just didn't happen in New Zealand. To add insult to injury I was told I would have to pay rent on the Elizabeth Arden flat which I had always assumed was included in the package. I told the manager I just wasn't having it and I was obviously fierce enough and persisted because I ended up getting it rent free.

At Bond Street we'd had a maid who melted our wax, another girl who made up our pads and patters out of cotton wool, another one who cleaned up after us; it was a very luxurious environment. Here in Wellington I was buried within a department store. I had a little waiting room, a treatment room and a tiny kitchen and I was expected to do everything: preparing the room, counting my laundry in and out, and sending the books back to London. The girls on the counter on the shop floor took my bookings and the money. At the end of the month, the store presented me with a cheque for two-thirds of what we had taken – they kept a third – and I sent it back to London. Every month it was out by a bit and I got a letter from Miss Milne the accountant – *Dear Miss O'Malley. I'm afraid you're threepence out by my calculations* – and so it would go on. It was hard work, a much bigger job than London and a very steep learning curve. But soon I found I liked the autonomy, I enjoyed being independent, it was like being in charge of your own salon.

My arrival had been well publicised and I was soon very busy. One day I got a call from one of the older assistants on the sales counter. She said that she'd got a woman who wanted to see me, but she did not feel she should be sent through. She lowered her voice slightly. The woman in question was quite well known to them: she was 'the bearded lady of Wellington'. Should the sales consultant just turn her away? I was horrified that she thought I would treat some clients and not others and said send her through, I would treat her the same as I would anyone else.

She came in; she had a thick growth of beard and a face very like a man's. She told me that she had read about me and she would like to have a facial waxing. I welcomed her but underneath I felt quite petrified. I got her into the treatment chair, covered her with a blanket and did everything I could to reassure myself that this was the most normal thing in the world. But I kept thinking, What if she is a he? What would I do? I told myself that they knew downstairs and started waxing.

I drew blood but she was so brave, she didn't complain at all. I did as much as I could and then I asked her to come back in three days when the skin had recovered. When she got out of the chair and looked at her face in the mirror she was so happy she had tears in her eyes. Suddenly she was ten feet tall. She had come in feeling like a freak of nature and I had made her look like a different person. She told me that she lived in the middle of nowhere and had gone to the public baths before she came to make sure that she was clean enough for me to treat her. She was a very gentle person and something about her situation touched me deeply. She became one of my regulars and no one gave me more satisfaction than that lady. On her second or third visit she told me that there had been a famous play some years before called *The Bearded Woman of Wellington* and they had got her to walk back and forth across the stage. No one had ever helped her before I came along. People had pointed and jeered and made a spectacle of her and all because of a hormone imbalance. When I left the salon a year or so later to take a transfer to the South Island I knew that she would be one of the people I missed the most. I hoped that she would go to see my replacement but I wasn't sure. She had very little money but she had found the money to come and see me. For the first time in her life, she told me, she could walk around feeling free.

My contract was for three years and I wasn't allowed to break it. But when a vacancy came up in Dunedin on the South Island I decided to take it. I did three weeks in the salon in Dunedin and one week in Invercargill which must be the nearest beauty salon to Antarctica. It was the most remote place I had ever been, but I loved it. In time I joined the local ski club and we had a lot of fun putting on dinners and going to fancy dress parties. I made the most of my stay there.

When my three years were up I went back to Australia and then on to south-east Asia where I did promotional work and trained the girls for six months before returning to London where I was immediately offered the best wage out to be a senior treatment girl at Elizabeth Arden's new premises in New Bond Street. I had hit the top of the company ladder but it just wasn't enough. The pay was still only twenty-five pounds a week and I had set my sights on buying my own flat and been recently turned down for a mortgage. I decided to call an old acquaintance called called Peter Ryan whom I had met years before at a cocktail party we'd had at the Cumberland. He was the manager of the Playboy Club and we had kept in touch.

He had tried to offer me a job before I went off to New Zealand but it hadn't been quite right at the time. So I went to see him and asked him if I could come and work at the Playboy Club as a beautician to the Playboy bunnies. I would do all their grooming. It was at the height of the club's popularity and the bunny girls were legendary. He said yes and another door had opened in front of me.

I enjoyed working with the girls enormously. Many famous faces came into the Playboy Club from film and TV; top sports stars and tennis players too. Eventually I made my way up to social secretary. I arranged golf, netball, squash, backgammon evenings; I had a budget of seventeen thousand pounds a year which was a huge amount of money at the time. The club employed 860 people and was making lots of money. Victor Lowndes, the owner, allowed the staff whatever they wanted.

One day Bunny Pamela came up to me with a mischievous look in her eye. She knew I wasn't seeing anyone and said, 'Do you want to meet a fella? He's not much to look at but he's got pots of money.' She must have known me better than I realised because she arranged a blind date for me with this chap called Steve Warrin and we got on instantly. He came to meet me at the club and I realised that she had seriously under-sold him. I thought he was a very good-looking man, well mannered, well dressed and a thoroughly nice person all round. He took me to dinner at a charming restaurant in Chelsea and from there we went on to Trader Vic's at the Hilton. It was a wonderful first date.

Steve was the first man I had met with whom I felt a rela-tionship could go deeper. And I didn't feel he was a threat to me. I felt ready for it; I had my own home and a career which gave me a confidence I'd never previously had. He was six years younger than me but he didn't show it. We met on an equal footing. He had his own business and played county golf but he wasn't rich as Bunny Pamela had billed him, our incomes were similar. I think that's why the chemistry worked: he was drawn to my independence. He helped me enormously when we decided to set up a golf society for the staff at work. I organised venues and once hacked around a golf course in a pair of jeans. I knew nothing about the sport and he stood quietly in the background, helping me whenever I was in danger of making a complete fool of myself. I went to a couple of matches with him when he was playing golf for the county. Steve played for England in the Boys International, and for England and Great Britain as a Youth International. He was also selected as a reserve for England in the Men's Home International Team.

During this time when I was enjoying the fruits of being a well-paid career woman living in London I decided to fly over to Dublin and see Mammy. I was there before she returned from a walk and when she walked in she asked Ian who the young girl was and he said, 'It's Kathleen, Mammy.'

She looked at me and said, 'I thought it was but didn't want to get my hopes up.'

After a while, back in London I received a letter from my mother asking if she could come and stay for a while. She had been ill and she wanted a holiday to get over it. I knew she'd had some sort of operation to remove a tumour but I hadn't wanted to think about it. I chose not to let the reality of how gravely ill she was get through to me on any conscious level. I didn't know what to say. Instead of seeing it as a chance really to talk to her for the first time, I just saw her coming over and being a nuisance and I couldn't face it. I still felt the embarrassment. I saw her making waves in my carefully constructed new life and, as ever, the memory of her visits to Moate came flooding back. But what was I so afraid of? I had my own home by this stage – I was no longer somebody's tenant. I should have welcomed a visit from my hard-working mother and shown her proudly what I had achieved and the flat I had bought for myself. I am so ashamed of this, it will undoubtedly go to my grave with me, but I was so fearful of an outburst I didn't even write back.

Not long after this Paul called. Mammy was in hospital and had been for some time. The tumour which had been operated on had come back and was getting worse. I flew home immediately. I could tell from Paul's voice that the situation was very serious. I spent a week with my mother and was there when she drew her last breath. I wish I could say that we had come together in those last few days and discussed all the heartache and grief and the big mysteries of her life but we didn't because she was too ill for any sort of proper discussion. Somehow, though, we did grow closer during this time, though the communication was largely one-way: we held hands and I read to her from books she found comforting.

One day the nursing staff got Mammy up for a walk. She'd had a stroke by this stage and she just said weakly, 'I can't,' swaying from side to side with the effort. After all the exertion she sat down on the end of the bed supported by the nurse and then she suddenly looked at me as though she hadn't seen me for a very, very long time. Her eyes were shining and she said, 'Hello, Kathleen, how are you?' Then she just slumped back on to the pillows. Those words were the very last thing she said.

The thing I regret most was the silence that persisted between us on so many topics. As a child I had loved her so fiercely, so totally, and then we had been separated for all those years. Worse than that, every time her name was mentioned at school it was in some derogatory or insulting way. *What can you expect from a woman like that?* Those nuns had not only robbed me of my childhood, they had robbed me of my relationship with my mother.

Mammy died on 8 May 1976. She died not knowing why the rather precious, fussy little girl who had been taken away from her at the age of eight had been replaced by someone so unemotional and apparently unfeeling. She died not knowing that her previously devoted daughters had been totally poisoned against her by the nuns entrusted with our care. She died not being able to speak to us as we could not speak to her.

Chapter 18

I wish Steve had met my mother. I wish I'd realised how quickly time was running out. She was fifty-six when she died and she should have been in her prime.

When Steve had suggested a trip back to Ireland, a year or so before her death, I managed to divert him to a weekend in Wales to spare myself any embarrassing confrontations. Yet if only they had known each other. Steve is such a handsome, presentable, caring person and it would have meant a lot to my mother to know that I had met a good man. He did not run away when I told him what had happened to me and my two sisters. He just said in his gentle way, 'Do you always make up stories about yourself?' I told him it was true and he just said, 'So?' He always felt that you can do nothing about which cards you get dealt, it's what you do with them that counts. He didn't really mind where I had come from, he accepted me for what I was.

I knew when I married him in 1977 that Steve had multiple sclerosis. He had a certain amount of wastage in one arm even then when he was in his late twenties. But we were together, we loved each other and were very much a couple when I found out the diagnosis. And at that age, one lives very much for the moment; it was impossible to imagine my fit, able, champion golfer boyfriend being anything else.

Nine months after we married I gave birth to our son Richard. He was six weeks premature and had to be delivered by emergency caesarean. Four hours after I gave birth, this little person dressed in yellow was handed to me and I thought: What do I do now? It was probably the result of all the drugs but I found it hard to bond with my baby at first. I held him and then he was off again, back to the Prem. Unit, and I was on my own. He was so early my milk had not come in at all and I seemed to spend a lot of time in those early days trying to encourage it out with the hand pump, anxiously hoping my body would start expressing naturally. I drank Guinness even though I loathed the taste of it – anything to get the milk properly established. Every time I went down to the new baby unit to see him, there was always one voice screaming out and it was always Richard's. He was being fed other mothers' milk and he wasn't at all happy. Then suddenly, on the second day or so, I went to see him in his little cot and he looked so frail and vulnerable and it was her eyes – my mother's eyes – looking up at me. After that, there was no going back.

Richard was sheer joy. I loved being his mother, but there is no doubt I made an anxious parent. I fussed over him and was always on the lookout for the slightest change. One time, when Richard was still a baby, I was staying at the house of my friend Sally who had worked with me at the Cumberland when he started to look a bit off colour. Sally was out and I had four-year-old James, her youngest son, with me. I said to him, 'Do you know where the doctor's surgery is?'

'Yes, I know,' he said.

So off we went on foot, with this little chap in charge of directions who unsurprisingly didn't have a clue where the doctor resided. We never did find it.

My son was fine, he was healthy, but *I* was neurotic. I watched his every breath. I wouldn't let anyone else look after him. We had moved to Pinner by this stage and didn't know anyone. We rarely went out because I was so worried about leaving him with a babysitter and something happening. We got invited to golf socials – to dinner dances and the like – and Steve would say, 'Let's get a registered sitter from an agency,' but I would worry all evening and wouldn't enjoy myself. Thankfully I improved as he got older.

Becoming a mother changed me. I kept the house spotless just as my mother had done. I was always scrubbing and wiping and polishing. I wanted the house to be as clean as possible for my child, just as she had wanted a clean tenement for her girls. I'd catch sight of myself in the mirror sometimes and my face would look just as my mother's had done and I would think, I don't want this, I'm not ready for it. I didn't want her face staring back at me; I still couldn't forgive her.

Most of the time I was just blissfully happy with my little growing boy; the world seemed full of possibilities again when seen through his eyes. Christmas had meant nothing to me for years, because it was the time when we were taken to Moate. It had been just another day, but with Richard it was full of magic and dreams. Suddenly I was able to enjoy it again.

The first year we moved to Pinner I had the strangest experience. I was just settling Richard into his cot when I heard exquisite celestial voices getting closer and closer. Suddenly I didn't know where I was any more. It was as though the clouds had opened and the angels were singing to me and my baby. *Silent night, holy night, all is calm, all is bright* . . . I picked up Richard in his blanket and went into the front bedroom where the sound was loudest, enveloping us in its sweetness. I was rocking my baby yet I was miles away, floating with those heavenly voices, transported to another world. I peeped my head round the curtain half expecting to see the angelic host in the flesh and there it was, the source of the ecstasy: the local Round Table had a float and it was driving past our front door playing Christmas carols at full volume. I was brought back to reality with a bang. I wasn't familiar with voluntary charity work, I didn't know such things went on in rural England. I had just heard the music and been transfixed by the joyful feeling.

When Richard was three years old, I went back to Ireland for my youngest brother Ian's wedding. Instead of stopping at the hotel where my entire family was staying in Mullingar, I asked my brother to drive me to Moate, about half an hour further away. I was still so brainwashed. I wanted to see the nuns and show them my perfect little boy and they would be able to see how well I had done. I wanted them to see that I was as good as they were. I dressed Richard in his smartest outfit: a white shirt, red velvet trousers and a matching waistcoat, and shiny patent leather shoes. I had my fox fur hat and coat on; it was my Sunday best, the clothes that I had bought specially for the wedding.

The Industrial School was no longer there. They had moved all the children out and the nuns were living in bungalows with a health visitor supervising them. The Kennedy report published in 1970 had been very damning of the entire Industrial-School system and the majority of them had since been closed down. This report had said 'even a poor home is better than an Industrial School for a child'. When I arrived Sister Aquin, who, apart from Sister Monica, was the only nun who showed any kindness to us, took us under her wing and showed us such great affection – love that she had not been able to show when I was just an orphan there. She doted on Richard and made it clear how much this visit meant to her. She was in her sixties now, but otherwise the same as ever: a petite lady, with fine features and a delicate voice. She hadn't lost her lovely slim figure at all. She showed me our old dormitory which had been partitioned off into smaller units, with two or three beds in each. This was used by families who found themselves in some sort of crisis and needed care arrangements, she said. But now all the children stayed together, brothers and sisters were no longer split up, hence the need for these units. All the time she was talking I just kept thinking of how it used to be with row upon row of iron beds and the freezing cold and no privacy and the girls crying into their pillows every night and the awful clammy feeling and the smell when you wet the bed. Did I imagine all that? It was hard to believe that it was the same room as the one in my memories with its new colourful furniture and jolly duvets. But Sister Aquin was halfway out of the door by now and asking me whether I wanted to sleep in the dorm or in her cell and I said in her cell which was a very nice room. I enjoyed being there, but the visit was stirring up a lot of old memories. That night in our little single bed I held on to Richard extra tightly as though I would never let him go.

The following afternoon, Sister Kevin came in whilst we were having afternoon tea in the priest's parlour. I had heard from Lydia that a 'serious' complaint had been lodged against her in the sixties. It must have been something very awful that she had done, because her cruelty was well known and everyone had just turned a blind eye to it. But she had clearly gone too far on some occasion and had only been allowed to stay in the order by the skin of her teeth. I was quite surprised that she came down to see me whilst I was there. She had always made her low opinion of my family quite clear.

They knew of my travels because I had written to them regularly, desperate for them to see that I'd got on in the world despite their attempts to make me feel worthless. But Sister Kevin took the credit for it: 'Haven't you done well because of us!'

So we drank tea together and on the surface it was all very polite and civil, but really Sister Kevin looked deeply uncomfortable now that she was no longer the big boss. Sister Aquin kept looking at me kindly though and I decided to push it a bit further and ask if I could see my school records. My mother had died some years before, but I still had so many questions I wanted answers to. There were mysteries about her life which I hoped they might be able to shed light on.

I said to Sister Kevin, 'Can you tell me something about my mother's background?'

'Oh, it's best not to bother because most of the mothers only took their girls back to make them work and skivvy for them. Your mother . . .' and there was a long pause. 'Best not to talk about it.'

She might not want to talk about it but I did. I had to know more. I had to ask, because it had been with me ever since she first planted the idea. 'Was she a prostitute?'

'Best not to talk about it,' she said, making it very clear that the subject was now officially closed.

I was left in that state again – just as I had been when I was fourteen years old. Not knowing. Feeling that they knew the truth and I didn't. But this time I felt angry as well. It really infuriated me that Sister Kevin, who had been reprimanded and stripped of her powers, who had been exposed as the cruel sadist she really was, still controlled the answers.

I didn't see anything wrong with my treatment for years. It wasn't until I became a magistrate in 1997 that the light really started to go on. And the more I sat on the Bench and listened to the terrible things that people do to each other, and heard words like 'abuse' and 'mistreatment' being bandied about, the more I questioned what had happened to me in my own child-hood.

Having blanked it out for so long, I suddenly started having vivid flashbacks. One memory played over and over again: coming up some stairs in the orphanage and seeing the door to the bathroom left open. Nothing unusual in that – we were never allowed any privacy – but there was a naked girl cowering in the bath and Sister Kevin had a pointer in her hand and was flogging this girl within an inch of her life. The girl was screaming, trying to protect herself. The nun was looming over her and beating her again and again. She was having to manoeuvre and manipulate that stick each time because it was so long and the bathroom was so cramped. It was a terrible scene. The girl was crying and crying for her to stop.

And yet I realise that it was a normal scene. I just looked at the girl without any emotion or compassion and walked on. I've looked back at that scene and wondered why I remember it so vividly. Sometimes I think it must have been me in that bath, shivering in the freezing water, trying to cover up my naked body, trying to shield myself as the blows from the stick rained down.

The nightmares came and with them more memories, strange pictures like disconnected film stills. I started to question how I had been brainwashed into believing that the people who had tortured me and robbed me of my childhood had done precisely the opposite – given me opportunities and made me what I was. More than that I questioned why I had aspired to be like them, to become a nun and join their order, despite the fact that over the years they had made it perfectly clear, though not in so many words, that I was not the sort they wanted to follow in their footsteps.

I had reinvented myself so soon after my arrival in England with stories of a nice middle-class boarding school in rural Ireland that I had genuinely started believing in it myself. Years of denial had followed. But now I puzzled: why had I always seen myself as worthless before? It was like the gradual shedding of a skin. The realisation that being me, the real me, not the invented one, wasn't all that bad.

Recently I spoke to my brother Ian about why I used to dash off to see the nuns as soon as I came back from England for the Christmas or Easter break. For years I did the same thing: spent a few days with Mammy, then rushed down to Moate to visit the nuns, taking all those neatly wrapped gifts (which they used to accept modestly and salt away back in their cells), desperately trying to prove to them I wasn't nothing after all. I asked him why Mammy didn't shake me to death to get some sense into me.

Ian was quiet when I said this. He'd obviously thought it all through before and simply said, 'Well, she didn't want to lose you altogether. And if that was what you wanted, she went along with it. Mammy was just happy with the time she did get with you. Her eyes would sparkle and her cheeks would flush at the very *mention* of you coming home.'

I've thought about that a lot since. The fact that my own mother didn't feel she had any right to say what I could or could not do. She had been told she was unfit to look after us and after years and years of being treated like a nobody, she had ended up believing it.

Until I became a magistrate all I had felt about where I'd come from and who I was was disgrace and humiliation. Everything to do with Mammy had been shrouded in a veil of shame, and she had died under that same veil. Now I was determined to delve into the past, to call up the records and find out who she really was.

Chapter 19

It had taken me more than forty years to wake up to what had happened to me as a child. For all that time, I had been in total denial about the 'reformatory' in which I had spent the majority of my formative years. I had taken Sister Cecilia's words quite literally and told only one or two people in the whole world where I had been brought up. I didn't want people to look down on me – who would? The religious were held in such very high regard in Ireland during those years, I knew that no one would have believed me if I had tried. But I wasn't alone in this. Many people in Ireland knew about the abuse that went on in the Industrial Schools but everyone just turned a blind eye.

I hadn't wanted to say anything because I was fearful that it would reflect back on my family and particularly on my son Richard. In contrast to my own schooling, I had sent him to a highly respected fee-paying private school and I didn't want to do anything to disrupt our nice middle-class life. But the more stories of trauma and abuse I heard in my work as a magistrate, the more I questioned why I felt such horror at hearing of children being beaten, when I didn't challenge my own beatings.

I had left Ireland at seventeen and made my home in England. Although I had regularly gone back to visit my mother and my half-brothers I was far removed from day-to-day events in Ireland and it was in the late 1990s that I noticed the sea change that had started to happen when people began to come forward and speak out openly and critically about the past. One day my brother called to talk about a programme he'd seen about the abuse at one of the Industrial Schools. It was quite a ground-breaking documentary and it had had a profound effect on him. There'd been other things too: a couple of the survivors had written a book about their experiences, there had been lots in the media about them. An action group called SOCA (Survivors of Child Abuse) had been formed and they were asking people to come forward. They were sending a team of solicitors over to Birmingham. They wanted to hear from people who had been through the Industrial-School system.

I was very nervous. Did I really want to go? After all, they couldn't change anything. I wasn't really sure I wanted to rock the boat at all. I went on the train alone and several times I thought about turning back. I walked into that room full of 'survivors' and it was a terrible place to be. It was full of the kind of people I had avoided for years. All the shame and the stigma of being Irish was in that room and it washed over me: *no Irish, no blacks, no dogs allowed* – the sign you used to see all over London. These desperate-looking people, down-and-outs and alcoholics, were what I had grown up with; they had all the degradation of the reformatory about them. They all looked as though they had a terrible story to tell.

The spokesperson for SOCA outlined the agenda: it was an action group for survivors to get the government and relevant religious orders to acknowledge their wrongdoing. Later some of the people got up and told their stories and though the meeting was chaotic, it was a start. I decided there and then that this was a journey I needed to go on. I hadn't enjoyed the experience one bit but I left feeling more elated than I had done for years. I was very scared about what the process would reveal but something in me was ready.

When I first spoke to the solicitors in Birmingham about my story they weren't at all sure that I had a case. After all, hadn't I had been raped whilst in my mother's care? Perhaps I had been removed from a dangerous background and the NSPCC were protecting me as they had always claimed. We talked it through and I left feeling very unhappy about this first interview. I knew that I had come from a good home and that my mother had exercised 'proper guardianship', but how do you prove that when it all happened so long ago? Then Ian called to say he'd come across something which might help. He was the only one of us who had not been removed from Mammy, the only one whose childhood was not interrupted, and he was determined to prove that Mammy was not a bad mother, but a wronged one. He now lived in Mammy's house in Dublin and he had decided to go through the attic to see if he could find anything of hers which would prove it. In a little silver box he'd found a letter from the Education Department saying she could have her two boys back. This turned out to be a very significant find because those boys, his older brothers, would still have been under five at this time and they would not have been allowed to return to her if she really were an 'unfit mother' as the authorities had always said. I showed this letter to my solicitor and then they knew they had a case.

While I wanted to proceed with my case, my greatest concern was what skeletons we might find in the closet concerning my mother. It had been so drilled into me that she was a woman with a murky past, or as Sister Kevin had so eloquently put it, a woman who 'walked the streets of Dublin', I greatly feared what I, or my solicitors, might unearth.

My solicitors applied for my educational reports but there was no joy. I went over to Dublin in 2003 to meet with the Commission, the body set up under the eye of Judge Lafoy to investigate and arrange compensation for victims. I said that I wanted to see the reports on my time at Goldenbridge and Moate Schools. They had promised us greater transparency and openness but in fact they were infuriatingly patronising about it and made it very difficult. In the end I returned to England empty-handed, but I persisted and persisted and in the end they agreed to send me the files, but they stipulated that I should have a doctor present when I read them. I called and said, 'How dare you? I lived through these experiences! Where have you been for the last fifty years? How traumatic is it going to be to read about them? Don't worry, I'm not going to jump off a cliff!'

When I finally got my school records the most upsetting thing of all was how *little* record they had kept of me. You could get all the reports of my Industrial-School years on to a piece of A4 paper and still have plenty of room left. The report on me in 1953, just over two years into my detention, simply says 'troublesome and unreliable'. Three little words – that was all they could muster on behalf of my year's education and progress; three little words to write me off. But when I read that I thought, That's not me: I finish what I undertake. I always have done. But perhaps that is what they did to me. They managed to turn a child who was naturally careful, a little finicky, a bit of a mummy's girl, into someone who was in their eyes 'troublesome and unreliable'. In my work I've seen enough of traumatised children to know that you don't go through what I went through without some fairly obvious psychological and behavioural problems. But it clearly bothered them very little. We were not worthy of being documented; we were non-people and so they did the absolute minimum. I could glean nothing at all about my primary education. These reports or lack of them sent a new wash of gloom over me. I knew that I had not received an education, but I had assumed there would be documents about me, even if they were lies. I had accepted that the nuns did not care about us but I hadn't realised that the educational body and the government had wiped their hands of us as well.

The Education Department have appointed the charity Barnado's to administer the legacy left behind by the Industrial-School system. They were chosen as an independent body, a non-biased, non-religious organisation who would ensure a level playing field, somewhere survivors could go where they wouldn't feel judged. They've sent me quite a few things, including the committal slip sending me to Goldenbridge at the age of five. All that's on it is 'Father dead'. And then on another form a simple word: 'Discharged'. Nothing more.

I got my detention records from Moate from the children's court in Dublin. I was taken down to the archives and shown these enormous scrolls, all just lying about on the floor. I went through by date and in the end I found it, dated 26 November 1950, and the reason given: 'Found having a parent who does not exercise proper guardianship'. It was signed Inspector Wogan of the NSPCC.

I've seen the committal papers for my two brothers when they went to Rathdrum. The reason given on those was 'destitute'. How I've struggled to understand that word. What is 'destitute' when you've got a roof over your head, hot food on the table and a mother to sing lullabies to you at night? What does it actually mean? I've read *Angela's Ashes*. That's poverty. We were never poor like that. The children in McCourt's book had no soles on their shoes. I've seen a picture of Paul and Bill from before they were taken away and they are two very neat-looking little boys in grey flannel shorts and shiny shoes and carefully parted hair. The more I think about it, the more I feel that 'destitute' had no precise meaning at all, it was just a statutory stamp for the committal papers – you either had 'parents dead', an unfit mother ('parent who does not exercise proper guardianship') or you were destitute. They were judgements entirely without legal or precise meaning.

The medical records which I got through Barnado's tell me nothing. They are full of empty phrases like 'dental treatment carried out'; 'all children have been immunised against diphtheria etc'; 'children are well cared for and happy'. That last comment almost made me laugh.

With every stage I've been excited. Each step unlocked another forgotten chapter. I've been on to the Sister of Mercy archives in Dublin recently, where the archives for the Industrial Schools are. Each time I've got my files I've found something else out. I got my school records. I was quite surprised to see I came out well above average in most of my exams. I got 165 out of 200 in maths. I was clearly not the fool I'd always thought I was! They actually broke it down for me and said I should have passed my Primary Certificate but because I didn't pass in Gaelic I failed the whole thing.

Research was fine, going to public gatherings of survivors was another thing. Somewhat reluctantly I went to another meeting in Kensington in 2003. The panel included the Irish Minister for Education Noel Dempsey, a spokesperson for the Commission and a barrister for the Redress Board, which organisation basically offered a shortcut to getting compensation without going near the other two. And there was a token nun. It was organised on Mother's Day; perhaps it was a quiet day for them or perhaps they thought they'd get fewer people attending.

It was a very noisy gathering as they always are; people were soon shouting and getting abusive. 'Feckin' get on with it!' 'Shut up, Mary.' 'Shut up yourself.' The survivors had no designated spokesperson because how do you nominate a representative when everybody is angry and hurting and everybody has a different story to tell? The panel were starting to make it clear that they felt the meeting was getting out of hand. One of them was talking behind his hand which I know from my magistrate's training is something you should never do. One of the survivors stood up suddenly. He'd had his hand in the air for the past hour or so.

'I've been here all day waiting for the money. Will you please pay me my dues now because I want to enjoy a few drinks at the Cock before closing time.'

Everyone laughed: we'd needed some light entertainment, but it signalled the end of the meeting, and you could see from the faces of the panel that it had turned out exactly as they had expected. But I felt so sad inside; it was just as it had always been: them and us. The meeting had fallen apart very easily. Those on the panel were clearly just going through the motions and the survivors, the audience, played up to the stereotype and confirmed the panel's suspicions that we were the dregs of society. It made us all look ridiculous.

Before the day had descended into farce the nun representing the Loretta order had stood up and offered counselling to all the people sitting in that room. It took my breath away. I was so angry I went up to her afterwards and said, 'Are you brazen or just stupid? How can you have the cheek, the affront, to offer counselling to the very people you abused? How dare you! You don't need to have a degree in psychology to understand how the survivors feel.'

She was quite surprised by this and started crying and said, 'I didn't do it.'

But I wasn't sorry at all, I just said, 'But you represent the body of people who did! And don't give me these crocodile tears – I've got years of anger.'

In due course my solicitor got the transcripts from Luke McCabe's trial. That wasn't very easy for me either. Thinking of my eight-year-old self in the dock across from that paedophile neighbour of ours, all I could do was shudder. When I first received the verbatim report of me being cross-examined I began to wonder if I had been right to stir the past up again. I had been doing all right in my life up till then. I was successful, grounded, had a strong family. I was tough – or so I thought. When the transcripts arrived I sat on the bed and I started reading them. But as I did so I had the curious feeling that I was sitting in the retiring room, in the magistrate's court, reading someone else's story. This wasn't me! I went through the motions of reading it, but it seemed so far-fetched, it was impossible to believe that it was true. I recognised it but it didn't seem to be me it was actually describing. I felt as if I were on the outside looking in.

But I read it again the following day and after a while the emotional barrier that I had put up as a very young child gradually began to lift and that was when I started to feel emotions again, honestly and directly; that was when I started to feel really angry about the damage which had been done to me and thousands of others by people who pretended all the while that they were acting in our best interests.

Of course this wouldn't happen today; we wouldn't make someone under age get up in a formal court situation and be cross-examined. If a child has to testify in court these days it will be 'in camera', they won't be exposed to a courtroom situation. The room that is used for family court is comfortable and familiar, more like a classroom than a courtroom. It is a very ordinary scenario designed so that children are not anxious or stressed out. Any testimony the child has to give will take place outside the public area. If a child has been abused he or she will usually be given a doll to demonstrate what has happened to them. How the child manages that doll will indicate to the psychologist or psychotherapist how the child has been treated. There is never cross-examination; there is gentle questioning. The professional counsellor will be looking to see if the child touches the doll in unnatural places or in an unnatural way. They can then decide in court without the child present whether or not they have been abused.

When I finally got my hands on my mother's files I discovered that the records on *her* were considerable. The Industrial Schools kept far more information on my mother than they did on us. Where she was, who she lived with, how she conducted herself on her visits: it was all there.

I came to one of the most recent entries first, the one that pronounced my mother sound enough to have her sons back at home with her. The precise wording describes her as 'a suitable person to be entrusted with their discharge'. But how and when did she become suitable? She hadn't changed her character. She hadn't changed her occupation. She still worked cleaning houses, cinemas, hotels, hospitals. The only thing that had changed was that she had married the boys' father. She had previously been unfit because she wasn't married and as soon as she was that changed everything. I have tried to understand how the NSPCC could take her children off her not once, not twice but on *three separate occasions*, then leave them without a second glance in places where they were abused. What angers me most about the judgements they made on my strong, hard-working mother was that she never failed to cope. She never went to the State asking for handouts. She was no simple-minded waif; she was perfectly capable of raising her children properly by herself.

Even when my mother was married to Paddy McNamara and newly respectable they continued to hound her. She had asked for our discharge and then suddenly withdrew it. After I was burned and she had started to press charges, she suddenly changed her mind and there is a note in her file on the incident saying 'no further action for the moment'. I believe they had threatened her with the possibility that, if she pressed the complaint, they would not let her have Sarah Louise when she reached her sixteenth birthday, which was imminent. But we weren't locked up for free. It was all there in the file: my mother had to pay for the privilege of having us detained under the 'parental moneys' scheme. This meant that single parents or poor parents were doubly stigmatised and punished for being unable to look after their own children. They were made to pay the State to take their children off their hands by handing over at least a part of their income. My mother received a widow's pension and an orphans' allowance of 13s 6d per week for the three of us. Some or all of that money went straight back to where it came from. Rather than paying the poor to help alleviate their difficult circumstances, the State took back that money which then went towards our keep at the Industrial School. And, by hounding her at home and work all the time we were away, sending in debt collectors to embarrass and hassle her, the State made very sure it was reimbursed every penny my mother owed it.

It's very hard to understand the morality of that time. I came upon the report of the Poor Law Commission of 1906 which laid out guidelines for treating women who had children out of wedlock. The men of course were not the subject of their concern for they had more than likely been tempted by the women in the first place, but the women . . . Their recommendations made a distinction between those who had a first child outside of marriage – they were 'first offenders' – and those who did so a second time – these were known as 'recidivists'. The basis for the distinction was that first offenders were in theory only slightly tainted, compared to those women who were supposedly incapable of being rescued and therefore needed to be confined for their own salvation. Furthermore such fallen women were perceived as doubly dangerous: not only was the unmarried mother a threat to the social order with her loose ways, but her child could be infected with the deviant genes and perpetuate that threat. So my mother was the creature that they most feared: a fallen woman who not only showed few signs of remorse, but had gone on to commit the same crime again four times.

Soon after the boys were taken from my mother she went to England, a broken and no doubt depressed person. But the files were still being kept. Where was she working? How much money was she earning? Was she married? Was she still claiming her widow's pension? She went to England to escape their endless persecution, the enquiries into whether anyone else was contributing to the home. They compiled vast dossiers on my mother. If they had spent half the time on my education that they spent prying into her personal life, I might at least have ended up with a minimal academic qualification.

I read my mother's file, particularly concerning those years in England, with a great deal of trepidation. But with every page my fears ebbed away. She was not a call-girl, she was a cleaner. She worked at Clerys' Tearooms and the Cumberland Hotel, a boys' boarding school in Essex and Woolworths. Did the sisters think she scrubbed and cleaned all day, then hung up her apron, put on her fishnet stockings and took to the streets? Why would she have done all that cleaning if she could have made a much better income on her back? I saw the addresses she worked at over all those years we were locked away; it is all carefully documented. This was a woman who did no wrong. They did all sorts of checks on her before she was given the corporation house in Raheny and it's quite clear in the files that she never even had a police record.

If my mother was a fool about anything, she was a fool about men. Paddy McNamara could have saved us from Moate and he didn't. He could have resolved everything by marrying Mammy and we would have been allowed home. But he didn't. He only married her when the boys were discharged and they had a third one on the way. For years I found the fact that he had it within his power to rescue us, but didn't, very hard to forgive. But it is possible that my mother didn't want to marry him. There's no doubt she was unconventional for the time and maybe she just thought, I won't have those nuns telling me what I've got to do in my own life! She had lost her first husband in tragic circumstances; maybe she had become cautious about relying financially and emotionally on a man at all. She knew we would be coming home at sixteen so perhaps she was just biding her time till then.

There is no doubt Mammy was in love with Paddy. You could tell by the way she looked at him that she adored him, and she let him get away with murder. Maybe he promised to marry her early on in their courtship and she relied on that? In the end she waited years and years for him to make an honest woman of her and for them to live together as man and wife.

A year or so before she died I gave my mother forty pounds to buy herself something. That was a lot of money in those days and I hoped she would buy a warm winter coat, something of good quality. Of course she didn't buy herself anything, she gave it to Paddy McNamara and he bought himself a new suit. I was enraged when I heard that, and I wrote her a letter telling her so. Even before I'd dealt with my past, I knew that Paddy McNamara could have changed everything for us and I deeply resented the fact that he was getting a handout from me. I didn't have the right to say what I did, of course; it was her money to do with as she pleased. I regret that letter now. In the end, however, he only wore that expensive suit twice and the second time was for his own funeral.

I have raked over my mother's life with a fine-tooth comb. There were no skeletons in her files. I have read everything they had on her and she was innocent of the crimes she was accused of. Whatever follows from this I can sleep easy and know that she was treated badly, she was the victim, she was the one who was wronged. *More sinned against than sinning* . . . Not long ago I realised that I had read every scrap of information the nuns had on my mother, I had turned over every stone and there were no secrets in her past, there was nothing to be ashamed of. It was only towards the end of writing this book that I realised what so much of the journey had been about – it was about vindicating my mother. As I write these lines I think, You're clear now, Mammy, and wherever you are, you'll be dancing a jig.

Afterword

In 2003 I was asked to speak on Irish radio. I had been invited on the show by Vincent Brown, a journalist and barrister whom I had become acquainted with, who was covering the *Pat Kenny Show* as a guest presenter. It was an hour-long programme; I spoke for a while then people were invited to ring in, and after my interview the switchboard was totally jammed.

After the programme a woman called Molly rang in; she was committed to Moate the same year I was discharged. She rang up because it had brought back a lot of memories for her. She was amazed to hear somebody for once agreeing with her story. She had had an awful time at the school, just as I had done, but afterwards our two stories departed somewhat. She had gone on to have a horrendous life. After numerous years of misery at Moate she was sent home to her mother who turned out to be an extremely abusive, sadistic person and she was treated terribly. She was forced to go out begging on the streets. She is now suing the nuns for dereliction of duty and lack of care in discharging her to an evil woman.

A man called in and said he had been at one of the schools

run by the Christian Brothers. He had ended up thinking that all the beatings and the fear were just normal. He still doubted himself. He was never shown any affection and it had had a lasting effect. He had very little confidence, didn't go out much and lived every day with a kind of guilty dread of being found out.

I heard from people who now, aged seventy or so, still wake up crying in the night, having nightmares about what happened to them. I heard from people who had been so indoctrinated with a sense of shame and low self-worth they have not told a soul where they came from or what they went through; one man said he had made a tape up for his family to be played after his death.

There was such an overwhelming response to the phone-in, Vincent Brown asked me to do a follow-up. He also – on air – asked the Sisters of Mercy to reply to my accusations. They took him up on it. He told me that they were going to challenge me. I felt nervous but glad the debate had really started. On the day of the programme Vincent got a call from a representative of the order. There was a big court case coming up so they were not going to respond to specific accusations at this stage. But they said to him, Kathleen O'Malley used to come and visit. She came every year to see us. Her sister Lydia married in Moate. They felt this was evidence which would discredit me.

'Most abused people return to their abusers,' I retorted. I had seen it regularly in my work as a magistrate; I wasn't having any of it.

Perhaps the most surprising person to call was the person who identified himself solely as my mother's brother. His message was simply that he would like me to phone. I was intrigued – perhaps this was the brother Mammy had once mentioned, the brother she had been split up from when she was six years old. I called back directly from the radio station and was surprised to find it was actually the man we used to visit in the Dublin Mountains – the man known as Uncle Terry. We chatted and the next day, still on a rollercoaster of emotion, accompanied by my stepbrother Bill, I went out to see him.

The door was opened by a much older man than I had known, yet although he was now well into his seventies, he was instantly recognisable as Uncle Terry. I was very pleased to see him but his reaction was quite extraordinary. He had obviously not made the full connection on the phone because when he saw me he just said, 'You were the little blonde girl with curly hair!' Then he broke down right there on the doorstep and cried and cried.

When he recovered himself enough, we went inside and I met his wife and we chatted pleasantly and had tea. We talked about Mammy and what she was like. As I was leaving he said when I came to Ireland again I must come and stay with them and he showed me the bedroom I would stay in. They were both so warm and welcoming I was delighted that going on the radio had allowed us to be reconnected again. We exchanged addresses and said our goodbyes. I wrote thanking them as soon as I got home. I wrote a Christmas card. I left messages on the answerphone. I wrote sending them a picture of Richard: I didn't hear anything.

Eventually I got through on the phone. I spoke to Terry's wife and she just said, 'Oh, you're the woman who came to see us.' She was very cold and I thought, Something has changed here. She made it clear that she didn't want to talk and just said that they'd got it wrong when I came to visit. She'd 'checked their records': my mother had left the family when she was ten or so and not nineteen as I had thought.

I have visited Uncle Terry twice since that initial trip and he has always been much more guarded. There have been no more tears. He drove me to the bus stop at the end of my last visit and said, 'I think this is the last you'll be seeing of me.' I wasn't sure if it was a reference to his ailing health or a desire to discontinue our friendship.

I've talked to my brother Ian a lot about this, about how emotional Terry was when he first saw me. My brother just said my face obviously brought something back. I do look quite a lot like my mother now and maybe it was the memory of her. I was left with the curious sense that I wasn't a stranger to him when I should have been. I will never know what it was that seeing me brought back to him.

I go to stay with my brothers in Ireland from time to time. It's lovely to talk about Mammy and the old days: it means a lot to me. I stopped at number 29 Lower Bridge Street the last time I went back. That part of Dublin near the Liffey has been pounced on by the developers and it's all very smart now. My old house is a very nice office. I spoke to the receptionist and told her I used to live there two floors up when it was a tenement and she looked quite surprised.

My sisters and I live at different ends of world. We have never really become close. We all invented different pasts for ourselves and kept well away from each other as we did so. There has always been a terrible silence about what happened to us at the Industrial School. I haven't seen my little sister, Lydia, in over thirty years. To this day she does not know about what Luke McCabe did to me and the reasons why we were committed to Moate. She was so young when she went in and we had not had the time to forge the proper bonds which should have tied us together.

The Industrial School left its indelible mark on my two older brothers as well. They were locked up in an institution which sounds even more bullying than the regime my sisters and I endured. It's no surprise to find that Ian, the youngest of my mother's children, the only one of us to have an uninterrupted childhood, is by far the most secure; he grew up happy, carefree, nurtured and loved by his two parents, his brothers and us, his stepsisters. As a result he is easy-going, successful and very family-orientated, the most balanced of all of us.

I was born a Catholic and will go to my grave a Catholic but the truth is I have very negative associations with religion of any sort these days. So much evil has been done in its name. I don't practise any more. That any religious order would do what it did to the children of Ireland's poor is beyond comprehension to me. Why did they go out of their way to make our miserable lives even worse? Why did they not do more to help us either spiritually or materially? Why did they have such low expectations of our levels of intelligence? The more I have come to terms with what happened to me, the less I have had to do with any sort of organised religion.

Yet I still love to hear the Mass sung in Latin: the nuns' beautiful voices raised in perfect harmony – that has a lot of powerful associations for me because it was so peaceful in the chapel. There was no shouting, no arguments, no beatings. It was a genuinely uplifting place. Not all of Moate was bad, just as not all the nuns were bad: certain people managed to transcend the brutal regime. Sister Aquin had a good friend called Sister Paul who was a gentle lady and a lovely person. She used to write to me and send me a little calendar every Christmas. Since I went on air I haven't received another one. Of course she has to stand by her community. She cannot be seen to support what I am saying. I can buy another calendar but I regret the loss of friendship.

I see a lot these days as a magistrate: speeding, domestic violence, youngsters with knives, shoplifting, drugs, vandalism and abuse. I love my work. It has meant everything to me to be selected as a Justice of the Peace. For them to have known everything and still chosen me is the greatest accolade of all. I spent so many years getting jobs under false pretences, it is such a relief being able to be *me* at long last. And I like to think I'm good at what I do. I definitely don't take anything at face value. Black isn't always black and white isn't always white. People aren't always what they seem. The most proper, outwardly decent people who have always paid their taxes can be doing terrible things to others behind closed doors.

I am lucky. I live in a nice sunny bungalow in Hertfordshire. I enjoy my work and in my spare time I'm a very active member of the local golf club. I was fortunate enough to marry a good man who turned out to be a wonderful father and a great provider even though the multiple sclerosis has taken its toll and he is now in a wheelchair. We are a very close-knit family, bonded in a way I and my sisters never could be. Our son Richard has been our life and he has turned out to be a wonderful young man. When I see him the sun shines.

Although I didn't have friends as a child and was cautious about revealing myself to people, that's all changed now too. I'm still friends with Sally from housekeeping and Nancy from the book-keepers' office at the Cumberland Hotel – they somehow got through to me despite all the barriers I put up. But it took me until Richard was thirteen or so really to open up to people and be myself. I had so much baggage I just didn't think anyone would really want to know me. These days I have some great friendships and I put a lot into it.

I've done a lot with my life but I feel I could have done so much more if I had been educated. I would have loved to study law or journalism but thought I would be rejected completely. All the years I could have done it, I just spent feeling worthless. Now I wouldn't be able to make the commitment because I have my husband to look after.

On a day-to-day level, there is a definite legacy of those years in the Industrial School. I'm frugal and I've become something of a hoarder: I save money, coupons, vouchers, old stamps. I can't bear to see nice things like wrapping paper being thrown away after only one use. My son laughs at me but I like to flatten it out – iron it sometimes – and keep it in a drawer for next year. Sometimes I take it too far. I have a girlfriend, Cheryl, who used to make beautiful birthday cakes for Richard. She made a whole range: castles complete with portcullis, teddy bears with knitted jackets on – they were so exquisite I wouldn't let him touch them on his birthday or the next day. Usually I made the poor boy wait about a week before he got to have a piece. She made me a cake once, pulled all the stops out for my fortieth birthday and, knowing what I was like, said, 'You are going to cut it, aren't you?' She could see by my face that I thought it far too lovely to destroy. 'Why do you have to save everything? Don't you deserve this cake which I've made for you?'

I just said, 'I can't cut into something that's perfect.' But I did.

There are some very dark memories to do with food. I don't think you ever forget that sort of gnawing hunger that we lived with every day. I've read of survivors who can't sleep unless there is a loaf of bread in the house. I'm certainly very frugal with what I buy and eat. In Moate if food had been left in the saucepan, even if it had been soaked in water, I would scrape it clean. Even now I will take a knife to a saucepan and eat the stuck-on bits. When I hear the harsh sound of the metal on the bottom of the pan memories come back to me. I feel guilty and grubby and even though I am standing in my nice bright kitchen in Hertfordshire I am back to being a starving orphan scratching around for any food I can get my hands on.

I like things to be clean and nice just as my mother did. And it is possibly no coincidence that I went into the beauty business – waxing and plucking and doing facials to make people feel better about themselves. At least I'm not as bad as one of my friends from the old days who washes her hands with bleach. She can't even get a cleaning job, her hands are such a mess.

I've had to learn to do things that would just come naturally to someone whose childhood wasn't interrupted and damaged. Before I was taken away I had a directness, an openness which I lost. I spent too long watching my step, keeping secrets, not speaking out of turn, trying to please, desperate to be liked. I wasted so much of my life with a great big chip on my shoulder – and it was all so unnecessary. It's coming back to me though. *I'm coming back to me.* And sometimes now I've started talking about myself, I find I can't stop.

I'm coming out of myself more in other ways too. One evening, to celebrate St Patrick's Day, I went to a dinner dance at my golf club. I got myself ready and then I got Steve ready. We went up there and it was lovely just as it always is. Then the dancing started. I didn't want my husband to feel left out so I sat with him and pretended I didn't care. But I love to dance. I sat there wanting to be on the dancefloor and started to feel rather sorry for myself. At some point though my friend Mary who was sitting at our table asked me to dance a waltz with her and I immediately thought, I can't! You're a woman – we'd look ridiculous! I can't dance with a female. We can't embrace! And then I thought, Sod it! Just do it! The realisation that I could do what I wanted, and not worry about the consequences or feel embarrassed or worried, as I had done most of my life, was a fantastic lesson for me – and I suddenly felt different. Mary got the music changed and we waltzed around the room and everyone smiled. Then the music went back to normal and I danced and danced and escaped into the music.

**You can order other Virago titles through our website: *www.virago.co.uk*
or by using the order form below**

☐ I Choose to Live	Sabine Dardenne	£6.99
☐ Slave	Mende Nazer	£10.99
☐ Desert Flower	Waris Dirie	£7.99

The prices shown above are correct at time of going to press. However, the publishers reserve the right to increase prices on covers from those previously advertised, without further notice.

Virago

Please allow for postage and packing: **Free UK delivery.**
Europe; add 25% of retail price; Rest of World; 45% of retail price.

To order any of the above or any other Virago titles, please call our credit card orderline or fill in this coupon and send/fax it to:

Virago, P.O. Box 121, Kettering, Northants NN14 4ZQ
Fax: 01832 733076   Tel: 01832 737526
Email: aspenhouse@FSBDial.co.uk

☐ I enclose a UK bank cheque made payable to Virago for £ . . . .
☐ Please charge £ . . . . . . to my Visa, Delta, Maestro.

Expiry Date ☐☐☐☐   Maestro Issue No. ☐☐

NAME (BLOCK LETTERS please) . . . .

ADDRESS . . . .

. . . .

. . . .

Postcode . . . . Telephone . . . .

Signature . . . .

Please allow 28 days for delivery within the UK. Offer subject to price and availability.